SLAVERY IN THE AMERICAS

Slave Rebellions

Robin Santos Doak

Philip Schwarz, Ph.D., *General Editor*

CHELSEA HOUSE
PUBLISHERS
An imprint of Infobase Publishing

Slavery in the Americas: *Slave Rebellions*

Chelsea House
An imprint of Infobase Publishing
132 West 31st Street
New York NY 10001

Library of Congress Cataloging-in-Publication Data
Doak, Robin Santos.
   Slave rebellions / Robin Santos Doak.
          p. cm.— (Slavery in the Americas)
   Includes bibliographical references and index.
   ISBN 0-8160-6136-X
   1. Slave insurrections — United States — Juvenile literature. 2. Slave insurrections — North America
   — Juvenile literature. I. Title. II. Series.
   E447.D63 2006
   306.3'62'097 — dc22

2005015722

Chelsea House books are available at special discounts when purchased in bulk quantities for businesses, associations, institutions, or sales promotions. Please call our Special Sales Department in New York at (212) 967-8800 or (800) 322-8755.

You can find Chelsea House on the World Wide Web at http://www.chelseahouse.com

Cover design by Smart Graphics
A Creative Media Applications Production
Interior design: Fabia Wargin & Luís Leon
Editor: Matt Levine
Copy editor: Laurie Lieb
Proofreader: Tania Bissell
Photo researcher: Jennifer Bright

Photo Credits:
The Granger Collection pages: Title page, 5, 23, 29, 31, 39, 41, 43, 71, 81; Associated Press page: 10; Library of Congress page: 82; Picture History page: 14; Art Resources page: 17; The Library Company of Philadelphia page: 19; New York Public Library, Astor, Lenox and Tilden Foundations pages: 45, 63, 65, 73, 92, 93, 95, 100, 104, 105; North Wind Picture Archives pages: 53, 76, 85, 97, 106; The Bridgeman Art Library page: 55; The Library of Virginia page: 59; Alan Hawes/The Post and Courier page: 68; Getty Images page: 87

Printed in the United States of America

VB PKG 10 9 8 7 6 5 4 3 2 1

This book is printed on acid-free paper.

PREVIOUS PAGE:

Slaves rose up against their French masters in 1791 in the Caribbean colony of Saint Domingue. After eight years of fighting, the French were defeated. This was the only successful slave rebellion in the Americas.

Contents

Preface to the Series

Philip Schwarz, Ph.D., *General Editor*

In order to understand American history, it is essential to know that for nearly two centuries, Americans in the 13 colonies and then in the United States bought imported Africans and kept them and their descendants in bondage. In his second inaugural address in March 1865, President Abraham Lincoln mentioned the "250 years of unrequited toil" that slaves had endured in America. Slavery lasted so long and controlled so many people's lives that it may seem impossible to comprehend the phenomenon and to know the people involved. Yet it is extremely difficult to grasp many aspects of life in today's United States without learning about slavery's role in the lives and development of the American people.

Slavery probably existed before history began to be recorded, but the first known dates of slavery are about 1600 B.C. in Greece and as early as 2700 B.C. in Mesopotamia (present-day Iraq). Although there are institutions that resemble slavery in some modern societies, slavery in its actual sense is illegal everywhere. Yet historical slavery still affects today's free societies.

Numerous ancient and modern slave societies were based on chattel slavery—the legal ownership of human beings, not just their labor. The Bible's Old and New Testaments, as well as other ancient historical documents, describe enslaved people. Throughout history, there were slaves in African, Middle Eastern, South Asian, and East Asian societies, as well as in the Americas—and of course, there were slaves in European countries. (One origin of the word *slave* is the medieval Latin *sclavus,* which not only means "slave" but also "Slav." The Slavs were people of eastern Europe who were conquered in the 800s and often sold as slaves.)

This drawing shows slaves carrying their master in a garden in ancient Rome. Slaves were a part of many societies from ancient times until the mid-1800s.

People found as many excuses or justifications for enslaving other people as there were slaveholding societies. Members of one ethnic group claimed that cultural differences justified enslaving people of another group. People with long histories of conflict with other groups might conclude that those other people were inferior in some cultural way. Citizens of ancient Greece and Rome, among others, claimed they could hold other people in bondage because these people were "barbarians" or prisoners of war. Racism played a major part in European decisions to enslave Africans. European colonists in the Americas commonly argued that Africans and their descendants were naturally inferior to Europeans, so it was morally acceptable to enslave them.

New World slavery deeply affected both Africa and the Americas. African society changed dramatically when the Atlantic slave trade began to carry so many Africans away. Some African societies were weakened by the regular buying or kidnapping of valued community members.

Western Hemisphere societies also underwent extraordinary changes when slavery of Africans was established there. Black slavery in North America was part of society from the earliest colonial settlements until the end of the U.S. Civil War. Many people consider the sale of about 20 Africans in Jamestown, Virginia, in 1619 the beginning of African slavery in what became the United States. American Indians and, later, Africans also were enslaved in Spanish colonies such as today's Florida and California and the islands of the Caribbean.

In early to mid-17th-century colonial North America, slavery developed slowly, beginning in Maryland and Virginia and spreading to the Carolinas in the 1670s. Southern colonists originally relied on white European servants. However, many of these servants had signed contracts to work only for a certain number of years, often to pay for their passage to North America. They became free when these contracts expired. Other servants rebelled or escaped. When fewer Europeans were available as servants, the servants' prices rose. The colonists hoped to find a more easily controlled and cheaper labor supply. European slave traders captured and imported more Africans, and slave prices dropped.

Soon, American plantations became strong markets for enslaved Africans. Tobacco plantation owners in the colonies around Chesapeake Bay—Maryland, Virginia, and North Carolina—and rice growers in South Carolina pressured slave traders to supply more slaves. In time, more and more slaves were kidnapped from their homes in Africa and taken to the colonies in chains to cultivate crops on the growing number of Southern plantations. Slaves were also taken to the Northern colonies to be farm workers, household servants, and artisans. In 1790, the U.S. enslaved population was less than 700,000. By 1860, it had risen to 3,953,750.

Similar circumstances transformed the Caribbean and South American societies and economies into plantation economies. There was a high demand for sugar in Europe, so British, French, Spanish, Portuguese, and other European colonists tried to fill that need. Brazil, a Portuguese colony, also became a thriving coffee-producing region. As the sugar and coffee planters became successful, they increased the size of their plantations and therefore needed more slaves to do the work. By 1790, Brazil was the largest American colonial slave society—that is, a society whose economy and social structure were grounded in slavery. Some 1,442,800 enslaved people lived in Brazil in 1790—twice the number that lived in the United States. Brazil's slave population grew slowly, however; in 1860, it was still only about 1,715,000. However, South American slaves were forced to work extremely hard in the tropical heat. The death rate of Caribbean and South American plantation workers was much higher than that of the North American slaves. Occasionally, a North American slave owner would threaten to sell unruly slaves to the West Indies or South America. Enslaved people took the threat seriously because the West Indies' bad reputation was widespread.

It is estimated that at least 11.8 million people were captured and shipped from Africa to the Americas. Many died during the slave ship voyage across the Atlantic Ocean. About 10 million survived and were sold in the Americas from 1519 to 1867. Nearly one-third of those people went to Brazil, while only about 3.8 percent (391,000) came to North America.

If the 1619 "first Africans" were slaves—the record is not completely clear—then there was a massive increase of the enslaved North American population from 20 or so people to nearly 4 million. In 1860, known descendants of Africans, both enslaved and free, numbered approximately 4.5 million, or about 14 percent of the U.S. population.

Slaveholders thought several numbers best measured their social, political, and economic status. These were the number of human beings they owned, the money and labor value of those people, and the proportion of slaveholders' total investment in human beings. By the 1800s, Southern slaveholders usually held two-thirds of their worth in human property. The largest slave owners were normally the wealthiest people in their area. For example, one Virginian colonist, Robert "King" Carter, who died in 1733, owned 734 slaves.

Consider what it took for slavery to begin in North America and to last all the way to 1865 in the South. This historical phenomenon did not "just occur." Both slave owning and enslaved people made many decisions concerning enslavement.

Should people hold other people in lifetime bondage? Could Africans be imported without damaging American colonial societies? Should colonists give up slavery? It took many years before Americans reached consensus on these subjects. White people's consensus in the North eventually led to the outlawing of slavery there. The Southern white consensus was clearly proslavery. Enslaved peoples had to make different decisions. Should slaves resist slavery individually or in groups? Should they raise families when their children were likely to live and die in bondage? Over the two centuries in which North American slavery existed, enslaved people changed their opinions concerning these questions.

Some white colonists initially tried to own Indian slaves. However, because the Indians knew the local environment, they could escape somewhat easily, especially because their free relatives and friends would try to protect them. Also, European diseases simply killed many of these Indians. Once European enslavement of American Indians died out in the 18th century, Africans and their African-American descendants were the only slaves in America. The Africans and their children were people with a history. They represented numerous African societies from West Africa to Madagascar in the western Indian Ocean. They endured and survived, creating their own American history.

When Africans began families in North America, they created a new genealogy and new traditions regarding how to survive as slaves. They agonized over such matters as violent, or even group, resistance—if it was unlikely to succeed, why try? By the 1800s, they endured family losses to the interstate slave trade. Black families suffered new separations that often were as wrenching as those caused by the journey from Africa. Large numbers of black Americans were forced to move from the older (Upper South) states to the newer (Deep South) territories and states. They were often ripped from their families and everything they knew and forced to live and work in faraway places.

This undated illustration of pre–Civil War life depicts African men being held in slave pens in Washington, D.C., about 1850.

There was only so much that African-American people could do to resist enslavement once it became well established in America. People sometimes ask why slaves did not try to end their bondage by revolting. Some did, but they rarely succeeded in freeing themselves. Most individual "revolts"—more accurately termed resistance—were very localized and were more likely to succeed than large-scale revolts. A man or woman might refuse to do what owners wanted, take the punishment, and find another way to resist. Some were so effective in day-to-day resistance that they can be called successful. Others failed and then decided that they had to try to find ways to survive slavery and enjoy some aspects of life. Those who escaped as "fugitives," temporarily or permanently, were the most successful resisters. Frederick Douglass and Harriet Tubman are the most famous escapees. Solomon Northup was unique: He was born free, then kidnapped and sold into slavery. Northup escaped and published his story.

Although inhumane and designed to benefit slave owners, slavery was a very "human" institution. That is, slaveholders and enslaved people interacted in many different ways. The stories of individuals reveal this frequently complex human interaction.

There were, for example, in all the Southern states, free African Americans who became slave owners. They protected their own family members from slavery, but owned other human beings for profit. One such black slave owner, William Johnson of Mississippi, controlled his human property using the same techniques, both mild and harsh, as did white slave owners. Robert Lumpkin, a slave trader from Richmond, Virginia, sold thousands of human beings to

Deep South buyers. Yet Lumpkin had a formerly enslaved wife to whom he willed all his Virginia, Alabama, and Pennsylvania property in 1866. Lumpkin sent their children to Massachusetts and Pennsylvania for their education and protection. He also freed other slaves before 1865. How could men such as these justify protecting their own families, but at the same time separating so many other families?

The Thirteenth Amendment ended slavery in the United States. However, former slaves were often kept from owning property and did not share the same rights as white Americans. Racist laws and practices kept the status of black Americans low. Even though slavery ended well over a century ago, the descendants of slave owners and of slaves are still generally on markedly different economic levels from each other.

The Civil War and Reconstruction created massive upheaval in Southern slave and free black communities. In addition, slave owners were often devastated. African Americans were "free at last," but their freedom was not guaranteed. A century passed before their legal rights were effectively protected and their political participation expanded. The Reverend Martin Luther King's "I have a dream" speech placed the struggle in historical context: He said he had a dream that "the sons of former slaves and the sons of former slave owners will be able to sit down together at the table of brotherhood." (Today, he would surely mention daughters as well.) The weight of history had already delayed that dream's coming to pass and can still do so. Knowing the history of slavery and emancipation will help fulfill the dream.

Introduction

Blacks enslaved by whites in the Americas were never content to be slaves, no matter how kind their masters were. Slave rebellions were one way that blacks tried to win their freedom.

The roots of slavery in the Americas stretch back to the earliest colonial period in the late 1400s. In 1492, Christopher Columbus arrived in the New World. Columbus, an Italian explorer, claimed the West Indies for the Spanish. He also gave Spain its first claims to parts of North, Central, and South America.

Columbus founded the first Spanish colony in the Americas on Hispaniola, an island that today contains the Dominican Republic and Haiti. He also established the practice of enslaving native people to work in the fields and mines of the new colony.

When the native tribes of the Caribbean were virtually wiped out by disease and overwork, the Spanish conquerors looked for another solution to their labor problems. They began working with Africans to kidnap and enslave African men, women, and children to work on Caribbean plantations—especially sugar plantations. The first slaving ships began arriving in the West Indies around 1502.

EUROPEAN COLONIES

Columbus opened up the Americas to exploration and colonization by other European powers. Before long, Portugal, France, the Netherlands, and England all had founded settlements in the New World. All of these new settlements relied on slave labor to grow and prosper.

The first slaves in English North America are thought to have arrived on a Dutch ship in 1619. With the establishment of English settlements throughout the 1600s—especially in the South—slavery took a firm hold in North America. From the mid-17th century, slaving ships brought thousands of kidnapped Africans into the colonies.

This illustration from *Harper's Monthly* in 1901 depicts the first 20 slaves being sold to colonists by Dutch traders in Jamestown, Virginia.

Before being enslaved, most men, women, and children from Africa had enjoyed freedom and independence. Some had been royalty in their homelands, others had been warriors, and some had led quiet, everyday lives raising their families. After enslavement, these people's lives were forever altered. In America, they became property, to be used and ordered about as their masters wished. Those who dared to marry and raise families in their new homes risked the heartache of being sold away from their loved ones.

ACTS OF REBELLION

The start of slavery in the Americas marked the beginning of slave revolts or insurrections. From time to time, for as long as slavery existed, slaves rose up against their masters. The first known slave revolt in the Americas took place in 1522, 20 years after the first shipment of African slaves arrived in the West Indies. Periodic rebellions continued throughout the New World until the end of the American Civil War (1861–1865). Slaves rebelled in Spanish, Portuguese, French, Dutch, and English colonies and in the American states.

Not all acts of slave rebellion involved outright violence. During more than three and a half centuries of slavery in the Americas, many slaves rebelled against their owners by using more passive means to protest their condition. Slaves often worked more slowly than they could have or pretended to be sick in order to avoid work completely. Some slaves lied or found other ways to quietly disobey their owners. Others destroyed tools, crops, and livestock.

Slaves had to rely on the food rations the master chose to give them. As a result, slaves were almost always hungry. To ease their suffering, many slaves stole food and goods. Others tried to escape, which was, of course, illegal. In the most hopeless of cases, some blacks chose to kill themselves rather than continue living in slavery.

THE EFFECTIVENESS OF SLAVE REVOLTS

No one can be sure exactly how many slave revolts took place in the American colonies and United States. Some historians count about 250 revolts involving 10 slaves or more. The exact count varies, depending upon how historians choose to define revolts and rebellions.

Slave revolts in the United States were almost always unsuccessful. They were usually crushed quickly after they began, and many of the rebels were put to grisly deaths. The fear of such uprisings caused white owners constant worry that there would be an uprising among their slaves. News of a rebellion in another colony or state was enough to bring about new laws aimed at restricting and controlling slaves. Even the whisper of a planned revolt was enough to paralyze an entire white community with fear. As a result, the atmosphere on many plantations was one of mistrust, fear, and unhappiness.

Perhaps most important, revolts and other acts of slave rebellion reminded whites that enslaved people were not contented to be treated like property or animals. As long as slavery existed in the Americas, slave insurrections continued to occur.

1

Slave Rebellions in the New World

This engraving from the 16th century shows African slaves producing
sugar for the Spanish on the Caribbean island of Hispaniola in 1595.

THE EARLIEST REVOLTS

The first documented slave revolt in the New World began in 1522 on the island of Hispaniola. In December, the slaves of Diego Colon, governor of the island and son of Christopher Columbus, rose up in rebellion on his sugar plantation. The rebellion was put down, and most of the surviving rebels were hanged.

Four years later, one of the earliest slave revolts known to have occurred in mainland North America took place in what is now Georgia. In 1526, about 600 Spanish settlers founded a colony on the coast of the Atlantic Ocean. The colony, San Miguel de Gualdape, was the first European colony on the mainland of North America. Within six weeks, enslaved people in the new colony rose up against their masters. Others ran away and sought shelter with the American Indians of the region. The rebellion, combined with disease, starvation, and Indian attacks, caused the remaining Spanish settlers to abandon the town and return to Cuba.

During the rest of the 1500s and into the 1600s, slavery became well established in the Spanish colonies throughout the Caribbean, as well as in South America, Mexico, and parts of Central America. As the numbers of blacks transported from Africa grew, so did the number of slave revolts. In 1537, slaves planned a rebellion against their Spanish masters in Mexico. In a letter to the Holy Roman emperor, Carlos V (Charles V) of Spain, Viceroy Antonio de Mendoza reported, "I was warned that the Negroes had chosen a king and had agreed amongst themselves to kill all the Spaniards and rise up to take the land, and that the Indians were also with them."

Although the rebellion was quickly squashed, other revolts would soon break out in the Spanish colonies. Escaped slaves in Hispaniola formed the first maroon communities. Maroons were fugitive slaves who banded together to preserve their freedom. On Hispaniola, the maroons became a powerful force.

The constant threat of rebellion and attack made the white owners uneasy and worried. In 1542, slaveholders told officials on Hispaniola that "no slave is reliable" and that the slaves "have more freedom than we have."

Although the first New World slave revolts began in the 1500s, slave mutinies aboard ships were not recorded until the early 1700s.

Other European nations—Portugal, France, England, and the Netherlands—soon founded their own settlements in the Americas. They, too, relied on slave labor to strengthen and grow their new colonies. The new arrivals soon learned the same lesson the Spanish knew: Any nation that enslaved people to work in its fields and homes ran the risk of slave rebellions.

In 1600, slaves in Brazil rebelled against their Portuguese masters in Pernambuco. The rebels overthrew their owners and fled into the mountains, where they formed their own slave community, or quilombo, called Palmares.

This maroon community grew to number about 20,000 former slaves. The quilombo was eventually destroyed by Portuguese forces in 1694.

The term *maroon* may come from the Spanish word *cimarrón,* which means "wild" or "savage."

In 1638, slaves on Providence Island, off the coast of Colombia in South America, rose up against their English masters. The following year, slaves revolted against French slave owners on St. Kitts, an island in the Caribbean. About 60 men and their families escaped into the mountains. The slaves fought off their pursuers but were eventually defeated by an army of about 500 men. The captured slaves were executed in horrible ways. Some were burned alive, while others were quartered, or cut into four separate parts. Their limbs were then placed on stakes and displayed throughout the island to discourage other slaves from rebelling.

Many of the European colonies that practiced slavery in the New World shared certain characteristics that increased the chances of a slave rebellion. These characteristics included the following:

• **More black slaves than white masters:** In most colonies, the number of black slaves quickly grew to outnumber the number of white colonists. In Jamaica and Hispaniola, for example, blacks made up more than 80 percent of the population.

• **A poor economic situation:** Slaves suffering from hunger, starvation, and disease were more likely to risk everything and rise up against their masters.

• **Large slave groups:** As many as 200 slaves worked on the large sugar plantations in the Caribbean. These large groups of slaves were more likely to work together to plan and carry out a revolt.

• **Geography:** Many areas settled by Europeans were large and wild enough for runaway slaves to set up their own successful maroon communities.

THE ROOTS OF NORTH AMERICAN SLAVERY

The beginnings of slavery in England's North American colonies date back to 1619. That year, a Dutch ship brought about 20 Africans to English colonists in Jamestown, Virginia. Jamestown, the first English settlement in North America, had been founded in 1609. It is not known whether the Africans were slaves or indentured servants, people who agreed to work for a certain period of time in exchange for their complete freedom. In 1631, the first slave auction was held in Jamestown, and 23 Africans were sold to the highest bidders. However, slavery would not become important to the colony's economy until the mid-1630s.

Virginia was not the only English colony to permit slavery. In 1641, Massachusetts and Connecticut passed laws making the enslavement of others legal. Slavery would remain legal in both colonies for more than 140 years.

In the early 1620s, the Dutch founded a colony in present-day New York and New Jersey. The colonists came to rely on slave labor to build their new settlement, New Netherland. The first slaves were brought into the colony in 1628. In New Netherland, the slaves were treated better than they were in other European colonies. For example, some were given "half-freedom." This meant that when the slaves were not needed by their masters, their time was their own. They could work and earn money for themselves.

In 1644, 11 slaves in New Netherland petitioned the Dutch government for their freedom. After the men agreed to pay a yearly tax, they were given their freedom, along with a small piece of land on the outskirts of the community.

Slaves in New Netherland were also sometimes set free or allowed to buy their freedom. These freed slaves could own land, marry, and pass their wealth on to their children. However, any child born to a freed slave woman was still considered a slave. Also, no matter how kind a master might be, enslaved people were still deprived of their liberty and dignity.

The first slave auction in New Amsterdam (which later became New York City) in 1655 is depicted in this late 19th-century illustration by the artist Howard Pyle.

COLONIAL SLAVE CODES

As the number of colonies in English North America grew, so did the institution of slavery. By the late 1600s, slavery was well established throughout the Americas. At this time, every colony in North America permitted the use of enslaved people to boost its growing economy.

For white colonists, a growing slave population led to increased fears of slave uprisings—and not without reason. By the 1650s, groups of runaway slaves had banded together and formed their own rebel communities in the swamps and forests near colonial settlements. Some wanted to be left in peace. Others turned to guerrilla warfare, attacking and raiding nearby plantations and settlements.

One of the first colonies to pass restrictive laws against slaves was Virginia. In 1662, the colony declared that any child born of a slave mother was also a slave. Three years after Virginia passed the law, officials there recorded the first planned slave revolt in the American colonies.

The plot, centered in Gloucester County, involved both slaves and white indentured servants. On September 13, the blacks and whites planned to rise up together. However, the plotters were betrayed by a fellow slave or indentured servant named Berkenhead. The would-be rebels were rounded up, and some paid with their lives.

As a reward for his actions, Berkenhead was given his freedom and 5,000 pounds (2,270 kg) of tobacco. Virginia officials thus hoped to encourage other slaves to report future rebellions. Officials also passed even harsher laws aimed at black slaves, including the Correction Law of 1669. The law stated that a master who killed a slave while punishing him or her could not be tried for murder, as the master would not deliberately destroy his own "property." Called "an act about the casuall killing of slaves," the law read,

> If any slave resist his master . . . and by the extremity
> of the correction should chance to die, that his death
> shall not be [accounted a felony], but the master . . . be
> acquit from molestation, since it cannot be presumed
> that [premeditated] malice (which alone makes [murder a felony]) should induce any man to destroy his
> owne estate.

The Virginia laws only encouraged more anger and resentment among slaves and maroons. In 1672, officials learned that maroons planned to rise up in small armed groups and attack plantations throughout the colony. As a result, the colony passed laws making it legal for people to capture and even kill maroons.

VIOLENCE IN NEW YORK CITY

By the early 1700s, New York was home to a significant community of slaves and freed blacks. After the English had taken New Netherland from the Dutch in 1664 and renamed it New York, they kept the institution of slavery firmly in place. In fact, many of the rights and privileges slaves had enjoyed under the Dutch were slowly taken away by the English. By 1682, for example, it was against the law for more than four slaves to gather together; two decades later, that number was changed to three.

In April 1712, a revolt of blacks erupted in New York City. About two dozen slaves gathered at midnight and set fire to a building. As whites arrived to put out the blaze, they were set upon by the slaves with hatchets, guns, clubs, and swords. About 12 white people were killed or seriously wounded.

The revolt failed, and the rebels were quickly captured. In all, 21 slaves were found guilty and sentenced to die. According to one account, one of the slaves was tried and acquitted twice before being convicted during his third trial. Authorities were determined to make an example of the slaves. Several were burned alive, while others were hung in chains and left to die slowly of starvation and exposure. To avoid this grim fate, several rebels who had managed to escape committed suicide.

After the revolt, the colonial government followed the pattern that would continue throughout the period of slavery: It passed restrictive new laws. One such law stated that New Yorkers wanting to free a slave must pay 200 British pounds (more than $33,000 today). This money was supposed to be used to support the slave if he or she could not find work, so the colony did not have to do so. The law seemed practical, but the cost of the slave's freedom was made so high to discourage whites from freeing their slaves.

Other colonies, worried by the recent uprising, followed New York's lead. To discourage the importation of slaves, Pennsylvania required slave owners to pay a high tax for each enslaved African they brought into the colony. Massachusetts banned the importation of slaves but did not outlaw slavery at this time. Massachusetts also passed harsh laws to punish rebellious slaves.

Officials in Charleston, South Carolina (called Charles Town at the time), passed a law that prevented slaves from hiring themselves out. This meant that slaves could no longer work for themselves during their free time to earn their own money. The practice of hiring out was common in colonial times. Now white masters in Charleston worried that slaves who worked outside the plantation would be exposed to radical new ideas that would lead to rebellion. The masters also wanted to prevent slaves from saving enough money to buy their own freedom.

REBELLION AND RUMOR

After 1712, officials in the American colonies continued to uncover plots and rumors of slave rebellions. In 1720, for example, a serious plot was exposed in South Carolina. Slaves in Charleston planned to kill their white masters and take control of the town. The plan was discovered, and the plotters were burned, hanged, or banished from the colony. An account of the plot, sent to King George I of Great Britain, stated that South Carolina's slaves "have lately attempted and were very near succeeding in a new revolution, which would probably have been attended by the utter extirpation (destruction) of all your Majesty's subjects in this province."

Officials in Virginia also uncovered several planned slave rebellions. In 1722, a conspiracy of slaves in two or three counties was crushed before it even started. The colony's lieutenant governor described the plot as "impractical" and "foolish." This might explain why the slaves at the head of the revolt got off easy: At their masters' pleasure, they were sentenced to three years in jail or banishment from the colony. The following year, however, the laws were tightened up: Taking part in a rebellion involving five or more slaves would now be punishable by death.

In the North, mysterious fires broke out in Boston, Massachusetts, and New Haven, Connecticut, between 1721 and 1723. In both cities, the finger of blame was quickly pointed at slaves. After executing one slave for setting a nighttime fire, Boston's lawmaking body passed a law that banned slaves from gathering in groups of two or more. Anyone who disobeyed the new law could be whipped.

THE MAROONS OF SURINAME

In 1726, slaves in Suriname, a Dutch colony on the northeast coast of South America, began a rebellion against those who had enslaved them. The insurrection would last for nearly half a century and result in one of the most famous maroon communities in the world. The escaped slaves built a number of fortified villages in the thick island forests.

After the initial revolt, 11 of the rebels were captured. Plantation owners decided to make an example of them and executed the eight women and three men in the most gruesome ways possible. Although the executions were intended to frighten other rebel slaves into giving up, they had the opposite effect. Rebels attacked and burned plantations around the colony, killing whites when they had the chance.

In the early 1700s, slaves who ran away from Suriname plantations faced an awful fate if they were caught. Upon the first offense, a runaway slave had his or her Achilles tendon removed. The second time, a leg was amputated.

The leader of the rebels agreed to a short-lived peace treaty with the Dutch in 1749. However, groups of rebels continued to look after the rights of those who were still enslaved. The plantations of particularly harsh slave owners were attacked and burned.

In 1757, the Netherlands tried to negotiate another peace treaty with two of the maroon groups. Four years later, a second pact was signed, and the groups were given their own territories. A Dutch report about the treaty stated, "All the negroes of the woods are acknowledged to be free, and all that is passed is buried in oblivion." At this time the number of maroons in Suriname totaled about 15,000.

The large numbers of slaves imported to European colonies in the Caribbean and South America were one factor in the higher likelihood of rebellions there.

Despite the treaty, the Dutch soon found themselves at war with other groups of maroons in 1772. The fighting began again because of the cruelty of the plantation owners. In Suriname, blacks outnumbered whites by about 20,000 to 1. During the fighting, the plantation owners were forced to rely on their own slaves for protection until Dutch troops arrived. They offered as many as 400 slaves their freedom if they would fight against the maroons. The Rangers, as the newly freed slaves were called, fought fiercely and managed to hold off the maroons until reinforcements arrived from Europe. The rebels were upset by the betrayal of the very men they were fighting for. They immediately executed all Rangers they captured.

Today, maroon communities still thrive throughout Suriname. These communities preserve the culture and many of the customs of the earliest African slaves. Maroons make up about 10 percent of the country's population. In 1980, they rose up in rebellion against an oppressive military government but were quickly put down.

British soldier John Stedman, sent by the Dutch to quell the revolution, spent five years battling the rebellious slaves. Captain Stedman later summed up what slave owners could expect in the future. "Every part of the world where domestic slavery is established, may be occasionally liable to insurrection and disquiet."

2

Fighting Back

When Africans rebelled against slave traders aboard ship, they were
sometimes thrown overboard and left to drown at sea, as illustrated in
this wood engraving from the early 19th century.

EARLY SLAVE MUTINIES

Many revolts took place before the slaves even reached the shores of their new homes. One of the first documented slave mutinies began on June 6, 1730, on a slaving ship en route to a Rhode Island slave market. Six days after leaving the coast of Africa, slaves aboard the *Little George* cut their chains and killed three watchmen. Over the course of nine days, 96 slaves battled it out with the *Little George*'s crew.

The crew tried vainly to take back the ship, throwing explosives at the Africans, firing the cannon at them, and even drilling holes into the ship to make it sink. In all, six Africans and five crew members were killed. The remaining crew members barricaded themselves below decks.

After bargaining with the remaining crew for their freedom, the Africans managed to return the ship to Sierra Leone, Africa, just a few miles away from where they had started off. They were guided to the shore by the captain, who yelled directions to the blacks from behind the locked and barricaded cabin door.

Slave mutinies were more likely when ships carried large cargos of people who had been abducted from the same village or area. These kidnapped Africans were better able to communicate and make a plan of attack. While most such revolts were unsuccessful, the slaves sometimes did manage to kill some— or all—of their white captors. Two years after the mutiny on the *Little George,* for example, Captain John Major of Portsmouth, New Hampshire, and his entire crew were killed during a slave mutiny. Such bloody battles for freedom continued for as long as the Atlantic slave trade existed.

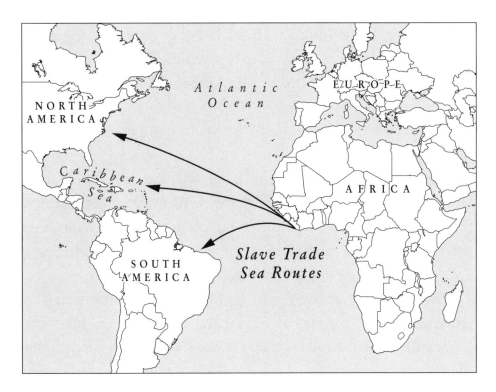

The journey from Africa to the New World lasted from 25 to 60 days. Many Africans took advantage of the long voyage to rebel against their captors before reaching their destination.

BLOODSHED IN THE CARIBBEAN

In other parts of the Americas, uprisings and rebellions continued. In November 1733, St. John in the Virgin Islands was the site of an uprising of enslaved people. The rebellion in the Danish colony was triggered by hunger and the harsh laws and cruel treatment to which the slaves were subjected. The slaves on St. John had to grow their own food to survive, but when drought hit the island, many of them began to starve.

During the revolution, about 150 slaves banded together. The rebels were aided by maroons who had escaped into St. John's wild interior. The slaves killed one-third of all the whites on the island and burned many sugar, cotton, and other plantations. As they moved from plantation to plantation, their numbers grew.

By taking control of the island's main fort, the rebels were able to hold the island for five months. During this time, they beat back two attempts by British troops to overcome them. Finally, in April 1734, French troops from Martinique arrived and put an end to the insurrection.

Two years after the revolt on St. John, British officials in Antigua learned that hundreds of slaves there were planning to rise up and kill all the whites on the Caribbean island. After the plot was revealed, more than 70 slaves were executed. Others were banished from Antigua.

THE STONO REBELLION

By the 1730s, the Southern colonies had come to rely on slave labor to drive their economies. An ever-growing slave population and news of slave revolts in other parts of the Americas added to the fear felt by white slave owners there.

To make matters worse, Spain, Britain's long-standing rival and enemy, controlled Florida. In October 1733, Spanish officials there announced that any slaves who fled to St. Augustine, the capital of Spanish Florida, would be given their freedom. The announcement was intended to stir up trouble in the British colonies to the north, and it succeeded. In the coming years, many slaves would escape from Southern plantations and head for Florida. Rumors of planned rebellions in the Southern colonies skyrocketed.

To protect themselves, South Carolina lawmakers passed the Security Act in April 1739. The new law required white men to carry firearms to church on Sundays, when most whites believed slaves were more likely to rebel. (Most blacks were allowed to work for themselves on Sundays.)

Despite this precaution, South Carolina's fears of a rebellion were realized in the late summer of 1739. On Sunday, September 9, a slave named Jemmy led an uprising in Stono, South Carolina, just 20 miles (32 km) from the colonial capital of Charleston. First, a group of about 20 rebels attacked an arsenal (a storehouse for guns and gunpowder). The rebels killed the two guards there and took the weapons.

At the time of the Stono Rebellion, slaves outnumbered whites in South Carolina by nearly four to one. In addition, the colony had recently suffered a famine, which created economic conditions that experts say made slaves more likely to revolt.

Next, the enraged slaves headed south. Carrying a banner with the word "Liberty" on it, the slaves marched toward the freedom of Spanish Florida. As they traveled, more and more slaves joined them. (Probably to avoid the horrendous punishments awaiting them, some later claimed they were forced to go along.) Soon, there were as many as 100 slaves in the group.

As the men and women marched, they burned several buildings and killed any white person who was unfortunate enough to cross their path. Adults and children alike were slaughtered. Only one white man was spared: an innkeeper named Wallace who was known to be kind to his slaves.

The rebellion did not last long. About 12 hours after the start of the insurrection, a group of armed whites overtook the slaves, who had stopped to rest in a field. The whites opened fire, and a fierce battle ensued. A report later stated that "one fought for Liberty and Life, the other for their Country and every thing that was dear to them." A number of rebels were killed during the skirmish, and the rest fled. Most were immediately captured; the rest were captured in the coming weeks and months. The captives were shot or hanged.

The revolt, the deadliest and largest in colonial America's history, resulted in the deaths of about 21 whites and twice as many slaves. It also resulted in the passage of a strict new law, commonly known as the Negro Act, in South Carolina. Under the new act, slaves could no longer work for themselves on Sundays and were not allowed to gather together in groups. In addition, slaves were now legally prohibited from learning to read. Southern slaveholders believed that literacy would only promote rebellion. The 1740 act also made the murder of a slave by a white person a minor offense, punishable only by a fine. The fine for killing slaves was less than the fine for teaching them to read. Another law rewarded people who brought officials the scalps of fugitive slaves. These new laws, which would be strictly enforced by Carolina residents, remained in effect for nearly 100 years.

Despite these new laws, slaves in South Carolina rebelled again less than a year later. The slaves banded together in an attempt to escape to Florida. However, the 150 men and women were soon captured. At least 50 of them were executed. Carolina officials hanged them in groups of 10 a day.

Rewarding Obedience

After the Stono Rebellion, blacks and American Indians who resisted rebels were given rewards. A document written in November 1739 describes the reward given to one such slave:

. . . a negro man named July belonging to Mr. Thomas Elliott was very early and chiefly instrumental in saving his Master and his Family from being destroyed by the Rebellious Negroes and that the Negro man July had at several times bravely fought against the Rebels and killed one of them. Your Committee therefore recommends that the [said] Negro July (as a reward for his faithful services and for an Encouragement to other Slaves to follow his Example in case of the like Nature) shall have his Freedom and a Present of a Suit of Cloaths, Shirt, Hat, a pair of Stockings and a pair of Shoes.

NEW YORK ERUPTS AGAIN

Slave unrest was not limited to the South. After the 1712 slave rebellion in New York, city authorities had passed laws aimed at preventing another such revolt. Almost 30 years later, however, the new laws had merely increased tensions in the city between blacks and whites.

By the early 1740s, New York City's slave population totaled about 2,000, while whites numbered about 10,000. As in other colonies, the growing numbers of slaves only fueled white fear. In 1740, slaves in the city were thought to be planning to poison the water supply. White New Yorkers bought bottled spring water from street vendors until the scare had passed.

By early 1741, white distrust of slaves was at an all-time high. In March, the first of a series of suspicious fires broke out at Fort George in New York. In the coming weeks, more fires raged out of control in the city. Many New Yorkers remembered the attack of 1712 and began to blame a slave conspiracy.

After being questioned, a 16-year-old white indentured servant named Mary Burton "confessed" that the fires were, indeed, part of such a slave plot. Burton blamed several people, including her white master and mistress, who owned a local tavern. Burton accused her master of planning to assist the rebellious slaves.

Over the coming weeks, Burton kept talking, adding to the list of accused plotters. At this time in history, the colonists hated and feared Britain's traditional enemies, the Catholic countries of Spain and France. Catholicism was even banned in New York. Soon, Spanish blacks and those whites suspected of being Catholic priests were being questioned. In all, about 150 blacks and 25 whites were arrested. Most of the accused denied Burton's accusations, swearing that they knew nothing about a black uprising. Others confessed after being tortured or offered a pardon and reward for their testimony.

Suspects were tried and most were found guilty. Thirty-one slaves were executed, as were four whites. Some of the condemned were hanged, while others suffered the agonizing punishment of being burned alive. About 70 blacks and a handful of whites were deported from New York, sold to plantation owners in Georgia. For her testimony against the "guilty" parties, Burton received her freedom and a cash reward.

As a result of accusations by 16-year-old Mary Burton, some people were burned alive as punishment for a supposed slave conspiracy in New York City in 1741.

The killings and banishments came to an end when Burton began accusing wealthy white New Yorkers—including one of the trial judges—of being involved. At this point, most people realized that at least some of Burton's statements were probably not true. Even during the trials, many New Yorkers debated whether Mary Burton was a good citizen or an outrageous liar. Today, the debate continues. Historians are not sure whether a revolt was actually planned or whether Burton's accusations just satisfied white suspicions.

THE VIOLENCE CONTINUES

In February 1763, a huge uprising rocked Berbice, a Dutch colony on South America's northeast coast that is now part of Guyana. In 1581, the Dutch had colonized the region, setting up sugar plantations and bringing slave labor from Africa. As in many other European colonies outside of the 13 British colonies, the number of slaves in Guyana greatly outnumbered whites. At the time of the 1763 revolt, the population of blacks in the colony was about 10 times greater than that of whites.

Known as the Great Rebellion, the revolt in Guyana involved as many as half the slaves in the entire colony. Triggered by the cruel treatment of slaves, the rebellion began on one plantation where slaves killed their overseer and a carpenter and burned down the owner's house. The rebels then marched from plantation to plantation, and at each, unhappy slaves joined the cause. During the rebellion, many whites were killed, and many plantations and fields were burned.

The uprising was led by a slave named Cuffy, a cooper (barrel maker) in the colony. Cuffy and his army of slaves eventually overthrew the Dutch government and took control. The rebels managed to stay in power for more than a year before being defeated by European forces. As the rebellion fell apart, Cuffy took his own life to avoid being tortured and executed. Today, he is considered a national hero in Guyana.

In the 1700s, Quakers were among the first whites in colonial America to champion the rights of enslaved people. Quakers were members of a religious group called the Society of Friends. In 1682, Quakers from England had founded the colony of Pennsylvania.

One of the earliest Quakers to speak out publicly against slavery was Anthony Benezet. A Pennsylvania colonist, Benezet became disgusted by the brutal practice in the 1750s. In 1775, Benezet and several other Quakers founded the first abolition society in America. (An abolition society is a group that worked to end slavery.)

In 1763, Benezet wrote a letter discussing the potential for revolt in the Southern colonies:

Should ye Almighty suffer the Negroes to become sensible of their State so as to rise upon their Masters, who can express the horror & distress the white inhabitants would be reduced to and indeed that this has not yet been the case . . . is certainly an unmerited Miracle of divine Kindness and Mercy to the Inhabitants of those Colonies, which there is no reason to expect the continuation of without repentance and amendment.

Benezet is shown teaching two slave children to read in the school he established in his home in 1750. Four years later, he started the first public school for girls in America.

MORE MUTINY

Rebellion at sea also continued in the years leading up to the American Revolution (1775–1783) as the transatlantic slave trade thrived. Most of these mutinies were not successful.

In 1765, several mutinies took place on slavers, the ships that carried slaves from Africa. One revolt occurred on a Connecticut slaver, the *Hope*. The ship was making its way home from West Africa when the enslaved people rose up. The Africans killed a crew member but were eventually over-powered. Seven Africans died in the struggle.

Another revolt occurred aboard the *Sally,* a slaver out of Providence, Rhode Island. The revolt began after many crew members became sick. The *Newport Mercury,* a Rhode Island newspaper, later described the rebellion.

> *The Captain selected a few slaves who looked more alert than the rest and allowed them to move about the ship at will, in return for their acting as crew members. The slaves freed their fellows in irons and rose up against the captain and white crew; the latter however, were armed to the teeth, conscious of the danger that free slaves on board represented; . . . [The captain] and his men met the attack with murderous fire, killing or forcing overboard eighty.*

By the early 1770s, war between Britain and its colonies was looming. Many slaves now thought they saw the opportunity to change their status from enslaved to free.

3

Slaves and Revolution

The 1794 convention to ban slavery in French colonies is shown in this engraving. This action by France increased pressure on other colonial powers such as England to ban slavery as well.

FREEDOM FOR ALL?

In the mid-1760s, British lawmakers had begun placing heavy taxes on many important goods brought into the North American colonies. Taxable items included tea, glass, paper, and lead. American colonists were outraged. Many people began talking about breaking from Britain and forming an independent nation.

On March 5, 1770, British troops shot and killed five Patriot rioters in Boston, including Crispus Attucks, a former slave who had run away from his master years before. Patriot newspapers dubbed the shootings the Boston Massacre and cried out for freedom. War between the colonies and the mother country now seemed inevitable.

As support for independence grew, abolitionists and former slaves took the opportunity to speak out for freedom for slaves as well. In April 1773, four Massachusetts slaves petitioned the legislature for their freedom—and the freedom of all slaves in the colony. The petition began,

> *The efforts made by the legislative of this province in their last sessions to free themselves from slavery, gave us, who are in that deplorable state, a high degree of satisfaction. . . . We cannot but wish and hope Sir, that you will have the same grand object, we mean civil and religious liberty, in view in your next session. . . . We acknowledge our obligations to you for what you have already done, but as the people of this province seem to be actuated by the principles of equity and justice, we cannot but expect your house will . . . give us that ample relief which, as men, we have a natural right to.*

In their petition, the four men spoke of their desire to leave Massachusetts.

We are willing to submit to such regulations and laws, as may be made relative to us, until we leave the province, which we determine to do as soon as we can from our joynt labours procure money to transport ourselves to some part of the coast of Africa, where we propose a settlement.

A runaway slave named Crispus Attucks became one of the first casualties of the American Revolution when he joined the crowd that was fired upon by British soldiers in the Boston Massacre.

The slaves' petition was ignored. Four years later, a former slave named Prince Hall and seven other blacks petitioned the Massachusetts General Court to abolish slavery. The petition resulted in a bill "for preventing the Practice of holding Persons in Slavery" that was debated in the Massachusetts legislature but not passed.

THE AMERICAN REVOLUTION

In April 1775, simmering tensions between Britain and its American colonies finally erupted into warfare. Out of fear for whites' safety, the Continental Congress banned the practice of arming slaves to fight for the colonies. The Continental Congress was the lawmaking body formed by the 13 original colonies in 1774. By this time, the number of slaves in some Southern colonies equaled or surpassed the number of white colonists.

The fear of an army of former slaves had taken firm hold even before the Revolution began. In New Jersey in 1772, for example, a letter printed in the *New York Journal* advocated sending all slaves to Africa or passing stricter slave laws. The anonymous author had overheard two slaves saying that slaves did not need to obey their masters, "for they would soon have none."

In September 1774, slaves in Boston volunteered to fight for the British in return for their freedom. In a letter to her husband, future U.S. president John Adams, Abigail Adams reported that the slaves had written to the royal governor of Massachusetts, Thomas Gage, offering their loyalty "provided he would arm them, and engage to liberate them if he conquered." Little else is known of the offer, and nothing came of it.

Even before the American Revolution, Abigail Adams pointed out the hypocrisy of whites fighting for freedom from Britain while denying blacks their liberty and rights. In one of her many letters to her husband, she discussed the 1774 offer by slaves to fight for the Loyalists. Then she wrote, "I wish most sincerely there was not a slave in the province [since] it always appeared a most iniquitous scheme to me to fight ourselves for what we are daily robbing and plundering from those who have as good a right to freedom as we have. You know my mind on this subject." People in Great Britain were even quicker to mock the colonists' double standard. British writer Samuel Johnson said, "How is it that we hear the loudest *yelps* for liberty amongst the drivers of Negroes?"

It did not take long for the Loyalists, or Tories (those who remained loyal to Great Britain) in the colonies to exploit white colonists' fear of slave rebellion. On November 14, 1775, Lord Dunmore, the royal governor of Virginia, issued a proclamation promising freedom to any slaves who deserted their masters and took up arms to fight for Britain. Thousands of slaves happily accepted Dunmore's proposal.

As intended, Dunmore's proclamation caused an uproar in Virginia. It also served to change the position of colonial officials about allowing slaves to fight against Britain. All the colonies but South Carolina and Georgia would rethink their slave recruitment policies, and about 5,000 slaves would eventually fight for American freedom. At the end of the war, most of these black soldiers were freed.

WARTIME REBELLION

As the conflict between Britain and the colonies heated up, more slaves than ever took advantage of the disruption to flee into the swamps and wilderness areas of the South. Some of these escaped slaves were trained by the British to fight their former owners.

During the war, rumors of slave insurrections—whether true or not—caused panic among colonists in Georgia, New Jersey, New York, North Carolina, South Carolina, Pennsylvania, and Virginia. Slaves were arrested, questioned, whipped, and sometimes killed.

The American Revolution ended in 1783 with slavery firmly entrenched as an important part of the economy in the Southern states. In the years to come, some Southern states would fight hard to hold on to the right to enslave blacks. In the North, the states would gradually abolish slavery, and more people would step forward to speak out against this inhuman practice.

Even after the war ended, some maroon groups continued to fight the Americans. In Georgia, for example, about

In the North, states began to abolish slavery during the American Revolution. The first to do so was Pennsylvania, which passed a gradual abolition law in 1780. (Vermont, which did not become a state until 1791, outlawed slavery in its 1777 constitution.)

100 slaves formed their own militia and dubbed themselves "the King of England's Soldiers." The escaped slaves attacked Georgia plantations and even took on state troops. The attacks ended in 1786, after the group's leader was executed. Through the mid-1800s, however, other guerrilla maroon groups would continue to raid Southern plantations.

The shaded areas show the locations of major slave rebellions that took place in the Caribbean and South America between 1500 and 1800.

SUCCESS IN SAINT DOMINGUE

In 1791, the only successful slave rebellion in the Americas began on the island of Hispaniola in the Caribbean. Saint Domingue, the western third of the island, had been under

French control since 1697, and the island was one of the richest in the region.

Large numbers of slaves were needed to work on the French sugar, coffee, and other plantations, and the bulk of these slaves came from Africa. By the late 1780s, the number of blacks on the island surpassed the number of whites by about eight to one. Though the French plantation owners were wealthy and contented, their slaves were not. The French were well known for their cruel treatment of blacks here.

When the French Revolution (1789–1799) began in France, the message of freedom and equality for all people spread to the colony of Saint Domingue. In August 1791, about 4,000 slaves in the northern part of the colony rose up, marking the start of a revolt that eventually spread over the entire island. The slaves were led by a religious leader and escaped slave named Boukman. Within two months, they destroyed hundreds of plantations and towns and killed more than 2,000 white colonists. The rebellious slaves suffered, too. During the revolt, more than 10,000 were killed. Many whites fled to the safety of the United States, where their tales of bloodshed and violence spread quickly to horrified slave owners—and awestruck slaves.

A former slave and carriage driver named François-Dominique Toussaint-Louverture became the most important leader of the rebellion. Toussaint organized the rebels into an effective fighting force. Under his command, an army made up of thousands of slaves took on and defeated Spanish, British, and finally French troops. By 1801, Toussaint and his army had taken control of the entire island.

Napoleon Bonaparte, France's ruler, sent troops to Saint Domingue to end the rebellion. The soldiers were partly successful. In 1802, they tricked and captured Toussaint. The great freedom fighter was sent to France, where he died in a French prison the following year.

The slaves on Saint Domingue continued battling the French for their freedom. In November 1803, the blacks triumphed, defeating the French soldiers. On January 1, 1804, the island was declared the independent republic of Haiti.

Haitian Hero

François-Dominique Toussaint was born in Saint Domingue around 1743. The son of a slave mother and a missionary father, Toussaint was born into slavery. At the age of 34, he received his freedom.

When the revolution on Saint Domingue began in 1791, Toussaint helped his former master escape before joining the rebels. After seeing how disorganized the mob was, he took charge. In 1793, he added the French word *l'ouverture,* which means "the opening," to his name. Toussaint chose the name to celebrate his breaking through enemy troops during one battle. Later, he effectively pitted the French, Spanish, and British colonizers against each other so that his troops could take and keep control of the entire island. Once in control, he moved to create peace between the victorious slaves and their former owners.

After he was captured by the French, Toussaint warned them that the freedom movement in Haiti would not be stopped. "You think you have rooted up the tree of liberty, but I am only a branch," he said. "I have planted the tree so deep that all France can never root it up."

THE EFFECTS OF THE REBELLION IN HAITI

The rebellion in Haiti had a tremendous impact. It proved to enslaved people that it was possible to revolt against their oppressors and seize their own freedom. Throughout the 1790s, slave rebellions took place or were suspected in Louisiana, New Jersey, New York, North Carolina, and Virginia. The coming years would bring some of the largest, most well-organized rebellions in the United States.

As in times past, white lawmakers and slaveholders in the United States decided that the best defense against a slave rebellion like the Haitian revolt was to pass new slave laws. In 1793, for example, the first Fugitive Slave Law was passed by the U.S. Congress. The law required that runaway slaves in any U.S. state be returned to their owners without any trial. The owner had merely to give evidence that the runaway was indeed an escaped slave. The new law resulted in many freed blacks being kidnapped from the North and taken south into slavery.

The rebellion on Saint Domingue also led white slave owners to decide that they no longer wanted to import rebellious or troublesome slaves from the Caribbean and Africa. Instead, they would rely on those who had been born into slavery, those who—presumably—would be more willing to accept their lot in life. In 1808, the importation of slaves was banned in the United States. The ban made little difference to Southern plantation owners, however, because by this time, the South had plenty of slaves available. These slaves—and their enslaved children and grandchildren—would endure the system of slavery for another 50 years.

4

Growing Violence

Slaves are shown removing the seeds from cotton with a cotton gin.
Technology such as this made growing cotton profitable in the South
and increased the need for slaves to harvest the crop.

THE MYTH OF THE HAPPY SLAVE

As the years passed, slavery remained an important part of the agricultural economy in the Southern states. By the early 1800s, importing new slaves from Africa was less necessary than before. A new generation of blacks had been born into slavery in America. Recent research has shown, however, that significant numbers of slaves were still being brought into the ports of Savannah, Georgia, and Charleston. Even after 1808, when the ban on slave importation went into effect, some slaves were still being smuggled into the United States. Even though people born into slavery had never known the freedom of their ancestors, many still rebelled against their enslaved status.

With their livelihoods dependent upon a slave economy, Southern slave owners needed to make sure that the practice of slavery remained legal. In order to avoid increasing criticism from abolitionists and others, slaveholders tried to create a vision of their human property as happy and contented. Slave owners often stated that slaves realized that they were well cared for and had better lives as slaves than they would as free people. Many slave owners tried to justify slavery by arguing that it brought Christianity and "civilization" to an otherwise "savage" people. Others portrayed the master-slave relationship as similar to that of a father and his children. These false images of slavery would persist well into the 20th century. In 1942, for example, a book incorrectly stated that "the majority of slaves were adequately fed, well cared for, and apparently happy."

In 1822, Edwin Clifford Hollis of South Carolina published a book aimed at convincing Northerners that slaves were satisfied with being enslaved. He included quotes from several plantation owners to "prove" his case. One said, "With humane masters, the negroes are generally as happy a people as any laboring class, perhaps, under heaven; and if I may be allowed the expression, an *inhumane* master, is a very rare character." Another stated, "In [the slave's] dreams, no visions visit him to remind him of his servitude. Born a slave, he need only be assured that he will be well fed and clothed for life, and worked in moderation, and he will regard himself as the happiest of mortals."

Idyllic scenes such as this one from the mid-1800s, which shows slaves dancing and singing, helped perpetuate the myth that slaves were happy with their plight.

Some Northerners who did not know any better bought into these tall tales of contentment, some of which were quite convincing. In 1853, David Brown, a "Northern man" who had spent time in the South, described a conversation between himself and his guide in St. Augustine, Florida, a 12-year-old boy named William:

I remarked to him, that all the negroes we met, seemed very cheerful and happy. He replied:

"Yes, sir; I believe they are almost always laughing and singing. . . ."

"But, William, don't they have to do a great deal of hard work?"

"No, sir; they always seem to make play of their work;—like those fellows yonder in the trees, picking oranges to send to New York, and throwing them at each other's head."

"On the plantations, William, they say the negroes have very hard work."

"May be, on some plantations they have to work hard; but I was out to Hanson's the other day to see them making sugar; and all the negroes seemed to make a frolic of cutting and toting the cane. I have seen some poor white men seem to work very hard; but I don't remember to have seen negroes seem to work very hard."

In the 1850s, a Northern minister named Horace Cowles Atwater toured the South. In a book he wrote about his experiences, Atwater exploded the Southern myth that slaves were contented and happy. He included stories of slave sales, beatings, whippings, and other aspects of life for enslaved people. In one chapter, Atwater discussed whether the slaves wanted to be free.

We were constantly told that they did not [desire liberty]. That they would not take it, if offered. . . .

Indeed, the owners ever affirmed, to me, that the care, the anxiety, the real toil was theirs. . . . If the slave is happy and contented, as we are so often told, what means that cry of insurrection—rebellion, which echoes forth from Maryland to Texas? . . . Rebellion is only to be feared, where there are wrongs to be redressed, and rights to be recovered. There is cause, why those masters should fear, and will ever be, as long as slavery exists.

The myth of the happy slave, however, was just that. Slave rebellions reminded white Americans that enslaved people were not content with their lot in life. These revolts displayed, for all to see, the obvious unhappiness of a life in bondage. During the 1960s, some civil rights activists would look to the stories of slave revolts for inspiration. Nearly a century after the end of slavery, the lessons of rebellion in the face of overwhelming odds were still strong and important.

To accept the myth of happy and contented slaves belittles the plight of slaves in America. Even slaves who were well-fed and treated with kindness were still not free. They answered to their masters in all things and were always at risk of being sold to other masters.

GABRIEL'S REBELLION

While whites in the North and South debated the happiness of enslaved people, slaves in the South took action to free themselves. These continued uprisings proved that the image of the happy slave was a lie.

The first revolt of the new century—and the largest the United States had yet seen—occurred in Virginia in 1800. The rebellion was led by Gabriel, a 24-year-old, educated slave who had been trained as a blacksmith. Hired out by his master to others, Gabriel came into contact with other slaves and free blacks. He came to more keenly resent the supreme power enjoyed by the white slave owners over their black "property." He especially hated his own master, Thomas Prosser. Prosser was known to be a cruel master who treated his slaves harshly.

Gabriel had heard stories of the 1791 slave uprising in Saint Domingue. The stories inspired him to take action. In the spring of 1800, Gabriel, his wife Nanny, two of his brothers, and other slaves began fashioning crude swords and bullets to use during their revolt. They planned to march on Richmond, capture the state armory and treasury, and attract slaves from all around. Their battle cry, they decided, would be the same as the one used in the Saint Domingue uprising: "Death or liberty." One rebel later stated, "We had as much right to fight for our liberty as any men."

After months of planning, Gabriel and the other conspirators were betrayed by two slaves, who told their masters of the coming rebellion. However, as many as 1,000 slaves still gathered at a meeting place on August 30, the planned date of attack. The rebels carried their weapons with them, and some were mounted on horseback. Their plans were ruined by a severe thunderstorm that washed away a bridge and prevented them from crossing a river into the capital. Had the slaves arrived in Richmond, they would have been met by about 650 men with guns, cannons, and other weapons.

An escaped slave is shown in this engraving from *Harper's Weekly* in 1864. Images such as this helped make people in the North aware of the plight of slaves and their efforts to escape.

As the rebellion fell apart, Gabriel fled. He was quickly captured in Norfolk, Virginia. He and 27 other slaves involved in the planned rebellion were tried and hanged. None ever betrayed the plot. Virginia's governor (and future U.S. president) James Monroe interviewed Gabriel and reported that "he seemed to have made up his mind to die, and to say but little on the subject of the conspiracy."

A British visitor to Virginia was told of the last words of one of the rebels:

> *A lawyer who was present at their trials at Richmond, informed me that on one of them being asked, what he had to say to the court in his defence, he replied, in a manly tone of voice: "I have nothing more to offer than what General Washington would have had to offer, had he been taken by the British and put to trial by them. I have adventured my life in endeavouring to obtain the liberty of my countrymen, and am a willing sacrifice to their cause. . . . I know that you have predetermined to shed my blood, why then all this mockery of a trial?"*

A Southerner later described the condemned slaves and made a dire prediction for the future: "The accused have exhibited a spirit, which, if it becomes general, must deluge the Southern country in blood. They manifested a sense of their rights, and contempt of danger, and a thirst for revenge which portends the most unhappy consequences."

Gabriel's Rebellion affected slaves and free blacks in other states. In the years immediately following the failed revolt, whites in slaveholding states were on alert, suspecting violence and death around every corner. In North Carolina, about 15 slaves were executed and others were tortured because they were suspected of planning a slave rebellion. In Massachusetts, where slavery had been abolished in 1783, a number of freed blacks were ordered to leave the state for fear that they were plotting a black uprising.

In 1800, the year of Gabriel's Rebellion, both Nat Turner and John Brown were born. The two would later lead important—although unsuccessful—slave rebellions. The same year, another future freedom fighter, Denmark Vesey, won a lottery that allowed him to purchase his freedom.

NEW TERRITORY, OLD VIOLENCE

Outbursts of violence continued occasionally throughout the early 1800s. In 1803, slaves in York, Pennsylvania, were suspected of setting several fires in protest after a black slave woman was found guilty of trying to poison two whites and sentenced to four years in prison. Whites in the town became so nervous about the fires that they ordered all blacks—freed and enslaved alike—to carry passes with them at all times.

In 1804, an uprising took place in the Louisiana Territory. This vast region had been purchased by the United States from France in 1803, nearly doubling the nation's size. The following year, slave conspiracies were reported in Louisiana, Maryland, North Carolina, South Carolina, and Virginia.

In 1811, trouble once again broke out in the Louisiana Territory. The revolt, the largest active slave revolt in U.S. history, took place 35 miles (56 km) outside New Orleans, the capital of the Louisiana Territory. On January 8, as many as 500 slaves from two parishes (counties) decided that the time for freedom had come. The slaves were led by a man named Charles Deslondes, who was later described as a free mulatto (a mostly derogatory term used to describe a person with mixed white and black ancestry) from Saint Domingue. Deslondes well knew of the victorious revolution in his homeland, and so did most other slaves in the New Orleans area. During the Haitian Revolution, many whites had fled the island and sought refuge in New Orleans.

Armed with such farming tools as hoes, axes, and knives, the slaves rose up and killed the son of a plantation owner named Andry. Taking all the guns they could find, the rebels marched to the next plantation. They moved from one farm to another, burning about five plantations and encouraging other slaves to join them. The ultimate goal was to capture New Orleans.

The insurrection, although large, was short-lived. The following day, the plantation owners banded together and began hunting down the slaves in the woods where they were hiding. Armed troops, sent from New Orleans, joined in, and many of the rebels were killed. Those who were captured were executed, including rebel leader Deslondes. Their heads were displayed on poles from New Orleans to Andry's plantation as a warning to other slaves.

5

Runaways and Rebellion

This illustration of slaves using dogs and torches to hunt other slaves
who had run away was published in a children's antislavery book in 1860.

THE BRITISH AND THE SLAVES

The War of 1812 (1812–1815) between the United States and Great Britain shifted white America's attention from slave rebellions to an overseas enemy once again. The war also raised the hope of freedom for many slaves. During the conflict, hundreds of enslaved men, women, and children fled to British army camps in the hopes of gaining their freedom. The British were only too happy to make use of some of these runaways, who were pressed into service in the British navy. The Treaty of Ghent that ended the war required the British to return all runaway slaves. Later, Great Britain had to repay the United States for any slaves that were not returned to their masters.

During the war years, unrest continued to plague slave-owning regions of the United States. White citizens in Louisiana, Maryland, South Carolina, Virginia, and Washington, D.C., all took special safety precautions as reports of slave rebellion surfaced.

After making peace with the British, the U.S. government turned its attention to Florida, now a British territory. For years, runaway slaves had found safety there, setting up maroon communities and living side by side with American Indians in the region. For this reason, many Southerners believed that the United States should annex Florida, or incorporate it into the nation.

In the summer of 1816, a group of about 300 fugitive slaves and 30 American Indians took over Fort Blount, an abandoned British fortress in Florida's Apalachicola Bay. After the War of 1812, the British had left the fort filled with supplies and weapons. The fugitives used the fort as a base of operations from which they carried out raids on Southern plantations. The fort became known as a haven for runaways, and Southerners demanded that it be destroyed.

Just days after taking control of the fort, the slaves were attacked by U.S. troops. The escaped slaves held the soldiers off for about 10 days. Then a cannonball fired by U.S. troops struck the fort's armory, causing a huge explosion that killed about 270 of the rebels. The rest quickly surrendered.

Even after the defeat at Fort Blount, several communities of maroons continued to thrive in Florida. Escaped slaves continued to raid plantations on the Georgia-Florida border. The raiding came to an end in 1818, when Andrew Jackson invaded the region and burned maroon villages and forts.

American Indians and black slaves joined forces in a number of battles against whites, as shown in this illustration from the 1800s.

In 1816, slaves in Barbados rose up against their British colonial masters. The revolt began on April 16 at Bayley's sugar plantation, one of the largest on the island. Led by a slave named Bussa, about 400 slaves burned sugar plantations around the island. Bussa, who had been brought to Barbados from Africa in the late 1700s, was eventually killed in battle, but the rest of the slaves fought on. They were finally overwhelmed by British troops. More than 175 slaves died battling the colonial troops, and over 200 more were later executed. Slavery was abolished in Barbados in 1834, 18 years after Bussa's death.

Slavery and the Missouri Compromise

In 1819, the United States was made up of 22 states evenly divided into 11 free states and 11 slave states. That year, however, a bill to admit Missouri into the Union as a slave state was introduced in Congress. People in the free states were outraged. If Missouri was admitted, the delicate balance of power in the government between North and South would be disrupted.

In 1820, U.S. politicians came up with a compromise. Missouri would be admitted as a slave state, while Maine would be admitted as a free state. The number of free and slave states would remain equal, and—most important—the looming crisis of disunity and civil war would be temporarily avoided.

The Missouri Compromise also made slavery illegal in any American territory north of Missouri's southern border (36°30' north latitude)—except in Missouri itself. The Missouri Compromise was repealed by the Kansas-Nebraska Act of 1854, which allowed settlers in new territories to decide whether they would or would not allow slavery. In 1857, the compromise was also declared unconstitutional by the U.S. Supreme Court in the *Dred Scott* decision.

DENMARK VESEY

In 1822, a free African American named Denmark Vesey tried to unite blacks in an uprising near Charleston, South Carolina. Vesey had been brought to the United States from the Virgin Islands when he was a teenager. In 1800, he purchased his own freedom for $600 (more than $8,700 in today's money) after winning a lottery. Vesey used the rest of the $1,500 prize to set up his own carpentry shop.

In the 1790s, Vesey had listened eagerly for news of the slave revolution in Saint Domingue. After securing his own freedom, Vesey became determined to lead the same type of rebellion in South Carolina. When asked why he did not return to Africa after he had bought his freedom, he replied that "he had not the will, he wanted to stay and see what he could do for his fellow creatures."

Vesey encouraged slaves to read Bible passages, especially those about the Israelites being freed from Egyptian bondage. He read abolitionist tracts and Bible stories aloud to slaves who could not read. Vesey was also quick to relate his own feelings about the condition of enslaved people. To convince another slave to help him, he said, "We intend to see if we can't do something for ourselves, we can't live so."

While spreading the message of freedom, Vesey began gathering like-minded slaves around him and planning his rebellion. Most of the slaves were field workers. House slaves were not trusted to keep the conspiracy a secret. Two of his helpers were slaves of the governor of South Carolina, and they secretly collected weapons. Vesey even contacted the president of Haiti, asking for military aid.

Denmark Vesey, shown speaking in this illustration, encouraged blacks to follow the example of the Israelites from the Bible who freed themselves from slavery in Egypt.

Some historians believe that by May 1822, Vesey had amassed an army of between 6,000 and 9,000 blacks who were ready to fight for liberty. The date of the attack on Charleston was set for a Sunday in July, when many whites would be outside the city. The would-be revolutionaries were to follow the same plan of action that was used in Saint Domingue: When the time came, the slaves would kill every white person they could, except the captains of ships. The rebels would force these white captains to take them to Haiti or Africa.

Before Vesey and his followers could begin their rebellion, however, their plans were betrayed by a house slave and other informers. The leaders were rounded up and jailed while awaiting trial. Inside the prison walls, Vesey told his fellow freedom fighters, "Do not open your lips! Die silent, as you shall see me do."

Vesey and 34 other blacks were sentenced to hang. Thirty-seven slaves were deported. Four whites were tried on charges of helping Vesey as well. The court also ordered that any blacks who wore mourning dress within a week of Vesey's execution should be whipped.

Denmark Vesey (1767–1822)

Originally named Telemaque, Vesey was a teenage slave in St. Thomas when he was purchased by Thomas Vesey, the captain of a South Carolina slaving ship. Noting the boy's "beauty, alertness, and intelligence," the captain allowed his young slave above deck and gave him new clothes. When the ship arrived in Saint Domingue, the boy was sold to a plantation owner. After his new slave suffered epileptic seizures, however, the plantation owner demanded his money back, and Captain Vesey took ownership of the teen. Renamed "Denmark" and taking his owner's last name, Denmark Vesey would spend the next 19 years as the captain's slave, until he bought his freedom in 1800.

Vesey married, had children, and established a good business and a nice home in Charleston. He was almost 60 years old at the time of his planned rebellion. He had been free for more than 20 years and was respected by blacks and whites alike. He could easily have chosen to live out his life in peace. Instead, he chose to take action against a great wrong by leading enslaved people in an uprising.

Vesey and five other men were executed together on July 2, 1822. Although the court had tried to keep the place of execution a secret, many blacks turned up to pay tribute to the failed leader as he went to his death. Fearing more violence, officials called in federal troops, and many of the spectators were attacked and beaten. After Vesey's death, officials buried him in a secret location.

The incident was downplayed by whites in South Carolina. The court, for example, stated that only a few hundred slaves had conspired with Vesey and that all had been punished. Newspapers in Charleston carried little information on the trials and executions. Even court records concerning the trials were burned by white families. White slave owners were worried that the records would incite slaves to more violence in the future.

In 1863, abolitionist and former slave Frederick Douglass recruited black volunteers for the Union army with the following words: "Remember Denmark Vesey of Charleston. Liberty won by white men would lose half its luster. Who would be free themselves must strike the blow."

DAVID WALKER'S APPEAL

David Walker was a freed black, a used-clothing seller in Boston. He often had slavery on his mind. In September 1829, Walker published a pamphlet called *Appeal . . . to the Colored Citizens of the World.* The pamphlet urged slaves to rise up against their white masters and fight for their freedom.

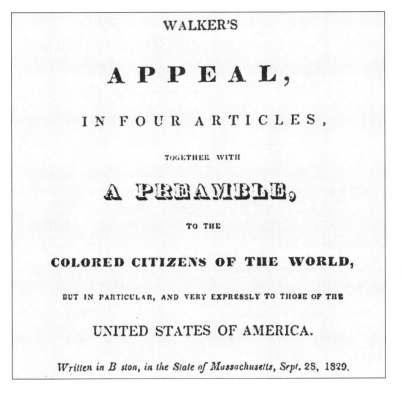

WALKER'S

APPEAL,

IN FOUR ARTICLES,

TOGETHER WITH

A PREAMBLE,

TO THE

COLORED CITIZENS OF THE WORLD,

BUT IN PARTICULAR, AND VERY EXPRESSLY TO THOSE OF THE

UNITED STATES OF AMERICA.

Written in B ston, in the State of Massachusetts, Sept. 28, 1829.

David Walker's *Appeal ... to the Colored Citizens of the World,* first published in 1829, encouraged slaves to take their freedom by force. This pamphlet was banned in many Southern states.

Walker's pamphlet was outlawed in many Southern states for fear that it would incite disobedience and violence. Despite the ban, many slaves did manage to get a copy. The pamphlet was circulated through Southern ports by sailors who supported Walker's cause. He often sewed copies of the work into the sailors' clothing. In retaliation, Southern states passed new laws banning the education of slaves.

In North Carolina, slave owners sent secret agents among the slaves to learn who had copies of the *Appeal.* A $1,000 reward was posted for Walker's death, while $10,000 was promised to anyone who brought Walker to the South alive. A year after the pamphlet was published, Walker, just 34 years old, was found dead in his home. While many of his friends and supporters believed that he had been poisoned, some modern historians think he may have died from tuberculosis.

Appeal . . . to the Colored Citizens of the World

David Walker was born in Charleston, South Carolina, on September 28, 1785. Because Walker's mother was a free black woman, he himself was born free. His father, however, was enslaved.

Despite his free status, Walker was keenly aware of the pain and misery his people endured in the South. He had personally experienced discrimination and prejudice while living in the North. Walker wrote his appeal to address slavery and injustice.

Now, I ask you, had you not rather be killed than to be a slave to a tyrant, who takes the life of your mother, wife, and dear little children? . . . believe this, that it is no more harm for you to kill a man, who is trying to kill you, than it is for you to take a drink of water when thirsty; in fact, the man who will stand still and let another murder him, is worse than an infidel, and, if he has common sense, ought not to be pitied.

Whether Walker's pamphlet was responsible or not, 1829 and 1830 were years of great unrest in some regions. On August 10, 1829, race riots occurred in Cincinnati, Ohio. More than 1,000 blacks migrated north from the city into Canada. The same year, slave set fires in Augusta, Georgia, and there was also unrest in Virginia.

6

Abolition, Religion, and Insurrection

This 1839 engraving is of Cinque, the leader of a slave revolt aboard the
slave ship *Amistad* in the same year. Cinque, whose real name was
Sengbe Pieh, was the son of an African tribal chief before his capture.

AN IMPORTANT ERA

The 1830s were a significant decade in the fight for black freedom. The beginning of the decade witnessed Nat Turner's Rebellion. Although the revolt failed, it inspired more outspoken opposition to the practice of slavery. White abolitionists and black abolitionists—many of them freed slaves—became more vocal and violent in their attacks on slave owners in the South. Refusing to accept any compromise, they insisted on the complete end of slavery in the United States.

In 1831, white abolitionist William Lloyd Garrison began publishing *The Liberator.* The weekly antislavery newspaper demanded an immediate and complete end to slavery. It would continue to be published until the Civil War. Garrison also founded an abolition society in Boston that attracted many members.

Black churches played an important role in encouraging abolition. The churches united both slaves and free blacks and spread the abolitionist message. Numerous slave revolts in the 1800s were led by slaves who had been inspired by sermons laced with abolitionist sentiments. After one failed revolt, a white man wrote, "Religion has been brought to their aid. Their leaders, who you know are preachers, have convinced many of them that to die in the cause in which they are engaged affords them a passport to heaven."

Those who supported slavery retaliated, punishing abolitionists and blacks who spoke out for freedom or trying to make the issue disappear completely. Southerners in the U.S. Congress, for example, were able to pass a gag order that attempted to prevent anyone from talking about slavery in Congress. In some communities, black churches were disbanded, and their leaders were banished.

At the end of the decade, the mutiny on the *Amistad* brought the slavery issue directly into the public eye. The *Amistad* case raised the question squarely: Were slaves human beings, with rights of their own, or were they property?

NAT TURNER

In 1831, the most famous U.S. slave rebellion in history took place. The uprising was centered in Southampton County, Virginia, an important farming region where blacks outnumbered whites. The revolt was led by a self-educated and highly religious slave named Nat Turner. In the early morning hours of August 22, Turner and other slaves traveled from house to house in Southampton County, using hatchets, axes, guns, and other weapons to kill white people.

The rebels spared no one in their path—young or old, male or female. Even infants were slaughtered in their cradles. The first to die were Turner's master, Thomas Travis, and his family. Turner, who described his master as a kind man, watched as his followers killed the family while they slept. He would later say, "It was my object to carry terror and devastation wherever we went."

As the slaves traveled from house to house, their group grew larger as other slaves joined in the carnage. House slaves held their masters and mistresses when they tried to escape. At the end of the bloodshed, about 60 whites had been killed.

This woodcut illustration from 1831 depicts the capture of Nat Turner following the slave rebellion he led.

Two days after the revolt began, it was over. Hundreds of soldiers from around the area marched to the scene of the rebellion. Blacks—guilty and innocent alike—were killed outright. Many were shot, while others were decapitated. In the coming days and weeks, about 100 Africans—many not even involved in the rebellion—were killed. Some were murdered by mobs of whites seeking revenge. Twenty-three blacks who helped Turner plan the rebellion were later tried, found guilty, and hanged.

Turner himself managed to evade those searching for him for several weeks by digging a cave underneath a pile of fence rails in a field. On October 30, Turner was finally taken into custody. At his trial, he pleaded "not guilty" because he said he did not feel guilty. He was, however, found guilty and sentenced to be hanged. While waiting in jail to be executed, Turner dictated his confession to a white lawyer, explaining his motives. He saw himself as a servant of God, sent to punish white people for the sin of slavery. He was hanged on November 11.

After the revolt, John Floyd, the governor of Virginia, blamed Northerners for inspiring and encouraging such actions. He especially blamed church leaders who had tried to convert slaves to Christianity and teach them about freedom and equality. Any organized abolition movement that had existed in the South was now doomed. Some towns passed laws that made it a crime for anyone to possess anti-slavery pamphlets.

The Life of Nat Turner

On October 2, 1800, Nat Turner was born into slavery in Virginia. As a young man, he ran away from his master. However, he had what he called a vision from God telling him to return to slavery. In the coming years, Turner had other visions of blood and human figures. He took these signs to mean that when the time was right, he must rise up against the white slave owners. He later said, "On the appearance of the sign . . . I should arise and prepare myself and slay my enemies with their own weapons."

In early 1831, Turner saw an eclipse of the sun. He believed that this solar phenomenon was just the sign he had been waiting for. He and a small group of his closest friends began to organize the rebellion. At first, they chose July 4, Independence Day, as the date for the revolt, but when Turner became ill on that day, the plans were put on hold until August 22.

More than any other before it, Nat Turner's Rebellion resulted in an overwhelming fear on the part of white slave owners. One Southern woman, a niece of George Washington, wrote in a letter that the atmosphere was like "a smothered volcano—we know not when, or where, the flame will burst forth but we know that death in the most horrid forms threaten us. Some have died, others have become deranged from apprehension since the South Hampton affair."

Abolitionists used the revolt to speak out against the crime of slavery. In an 1860 book about slave insurrections, abolitionist Joshua Coffin prefaced his catalog with the following warning: "[Slave rebellions] exhibit clearly the dangers to which slaveholders are always liable, as well as the safety of immediate emancipation. They furnish, in both cases, a rule which admits of no exception, as it is always dangerous to do wrong, and safe to do right."

The Turner Rebellion caused Virginia lawmakers to argue the benefits of abolishing slavery. Others suggested setting up a fund that would allow freed blacks to be sent out of the country. After the revolt, Maryland did in fact establish a society to raise funds to send freed blacks to Liberia in Africa. Liberia had been founded in 1821 as a home for freed slaves.

As usual, however, the actual response was to pass legislation aimed at further restricting the very few freedoms blacks in Virginia enjoyed. In 1831 and 1832, blacks were banned from holding religious meetings or preaching to groups of blacks. They could not carry weapons or buy alcohol. In Maryland, state officials tightened up on a law that prevented freed blacks from settling there. Any slave owner in Maryland who chose to free slaves had to send them out of state.

UNREST EVERYWHERE

The 1830s were a time of great unrest elsewhere in the Americas. In December 1831, for example, the Great Slave Revolt occurred in Jamaica. At this time, Jamaica was a British colony where slaves outnumbered whites by about ten to one.

The rebellion began when a rumor spread among the 300,000 slaves on the island that King William IV of Great Britain had abolished slavery. When colonial officials tried to deny the slaves their freedom, they rose up under the leadership of a Baptist preacher named Samuel Sharpe. Although Sharpe had planned a work strike (a stoppage of work in order to get better conditions or pay), the peaceful protest soon turned violent. During the revolt, more than 150 plantations were burned, and about 14 whites were killed.

Born in Jamaica, Samuel Sharpe was a 31-year-old field slave at the time of the uprising. Before his death, he said, "I would rather die upon yonder gallows than live in slavery." Today, Sharpe is remembered on Jamaica's National Heroes Day each October.

The revolt was put down after eight days by British troops. Rebellious slaves were captured and harshly punished. According to some estimates, as many as 500 slaves were executed, and their homes and property were burned. Sharpe was among those killed after the revolt.

Although the rebellion had failed, it encouraged law-makers in Great Britain to consider putting an end to slavery in their colonies. In 1833, two years after the revolt in Jamaica, Parliament, Britain's lawmaking body, voted to end slavery throughout the British Empire.

In 1835, a slave revolt began in northern Brazil. Called the Cabanagem Revolt, the rebellion was led by Muslims who had been enslaved and brought from Africa. During the revolt, which lasted nearly two years, whites were butchered. After the rebellion was suppressed, Brazilian officials tried to deport all freed blacks in the country. Under pressure from Great Britain, Brazil finally abolished the slave trade in 1851.

THE *AMISTAD*

In the summer of 1839, an incident occurred at sea that would force Americans to confront the issue of slavery head-on. In early July, the Spanish slave ship *Amistad* was on its way from Havana, Cuba, to a sugar plantation at Puerto Principe, a part of Cuba about 300 miles (480 km) away. The ship's cargo included 53 Africans that two men in Cuba claimed as slaves—49 adult males and four children.

One of the Africans, Sengbe Pieh, was the son of a Mende chief in present-day Sierra Leone, Africa. Back home, Sengbe had been a rice farmer with a wife and three children. Kidnapped by slave traders, he was taken to Havana, renamed Cinque by his captors, and sold off to a planter. Now, he found himself huddled together with other captives aboard the *Amistad*, on their way to a lifetime of labor and misery.

In this wood engraving from 1840, African slaves, led by Cinque, kill Captain Ramon Ferrer during the 1839 insurrection on board the Spanish slave ship *Amistad*.

A revolt led by Cinque began after the ship's cook pointed at the Africans and then at a barrel of salted meat. The slaves took this to mean that the crew was going to kill and cook them. In the early morning hours of July 2, Cinque and the other Africans managed to free themselves and attacked the ship's crew with sugarcane knives they found in the hold. During the rebellion, the Africans killed the cook and the ship's captain. The ship's two crew members dived overboard to spare themselves the same fate. The only whites left on board the ship were the 16-year-old cabin boy and the two plantation owners, José Ruiz and Pedro Montes, the men who had purchased the cargo of slaves in Havana. Two of the slaves were also killed during their battle for freedom.

The Africans ordered the plantation owners to return the ship to West Africa. Cinque told Ruiz and Montes to sail into the rising sun. During the day, the two Cubans complied, but at night, they turned the ship north, sailing further and further from Africa. By doing this, the two captives hoped to be spotted and rescued by a passing ship.

Former president John Quincy Adams, shown here, successfully argued that the Africans from the *Amistad* should be free men. They were granted their freedom in early 1841.

On August 25, after nearly two months at sea, the *Amistad* reached Long Island, New York. Eight of the Africans had died from disease or exposure during the trip. The survivors were thin and ill. Here, the ship was seized by the United States and towed to New London, Connecticut, where Ruiz and Montes told their tale of mutiny and murder. Although the two men asked for their "property" back, Connecticut officials were unsure what to do. They decided that the matter must be handled in court and sent the surviving Africans to await trial in a New Haven jail.

During the Africans' time in jail, abolitionists taught them some English and tried to convert them to Christianity. Some of the Africans wrote letters from jail to their lawyer, former U.S. president John Quincy Adams. One Mende named Kale wrote,

We want you to ask the Court what we have done wrong. What for Americans keep us in prison. Some people say Mendi people crazy, Mendi people dolt, because we no talk America language.

America people no talk Mendi language. American people crazy dolts? . . .

Dear friend Mr. Adams, you have children, you have friends, you love them, you feel very sorry if Mendi people come and take all to Africa. We feel bad for our friends, and our friends all feel bad for us. . . . Dear friend, we want you to know how we feel. Mendi people think, think, think. *Nobody know what we think. . . . Mendi people have got souls.*

Abolitionists immediately began publicizing the *Amistad* story, making heroes out of the Africans who had fought for their own liberty against all odds. Northern sentiment quickly turned against the Spanish slaveholders. Less than a month after the Africans arrived in the United States, a play about the *Amistad* revolt, called *The Black Schooner*, was staged in New York. Later, a wax exhibit featuring the Africans appeared at a New York museum.

Northern abolitionists also formed the Amistad Committee to raise funds for the Africans' defense. The committee managed to have Ruiz and Montes arrested in New York for false imprisonment, assault, and battery. When the men were released from jail a week later, they fled to Cuba.

U.S. president Martin Van Buren did not want to start trouble with Spain. He agreed with Spanish authorities that the Africans should be sent back to Cuba and put on trial for mutiny and murder. However, a U.S. judge in Connecticut ruled that the Africans need not be returned to the Spanish.

The case was appealed by the Spanish and U.S. governments in the U.S. Supreme Court. Here, former president John Quincy Adams took up the Africans' cause. He forcefully argued that the men had been illegally kidnapped from their homes in Africa. In early 1841, more than a year after they had arrived on U.S. soil, the Africans got their final day in court. The Supreme Court justices ruled that the men and children indeed were and had been free and should be returned to their homes in Africa.

In January 1842, the 35 slaves who had survived their ordeal in the United States went home to Sierra Leone. During the time they had spent in America, they had toured New England in an effort to raise the money for the passage home, since the administration of President Van Buren refused to give the slaves any assistance. After arriving home, Sengbe learned that his family had been killed or kidnapped in "slaving wars." He never saw them again.

7

Reaching a Boiling Point

Slave auctions such as this one in New Orleans, Louisiana, were common throughout the South. The treatment of African Americans as property to be bought and sold fueled rebellion among slaves.

BEFORE THE WAR

The period leading up to the Civil War saw continued violent rebellion in the South. One hot spot at this time was Louisiana. Since the 1830s, slave plots and maroon bands in Cypress Swamp had caused nearly constant problems and worries for local plantation owners.

In the fall of 1840, an uprising in several Louisiana parishes was uncovered. Hundreds of slaves—as well as some "white abolition rascals"—were thought to be involved. After the revolt was revealed, slaves (both guilty and innocent) were imprisoned, whipped, and executed.

Such plots, whether real or imagined, continued to create panic in Louisiana and other Southern states. In New Orleans in 1841, a newspaper editorial claimed that the trouble between slave and master was "rapidly maturing." The writer continued, "Let us always be on our guard, and grant no indulgences to the negro, but keep him strictly within his sphere."

MUTINY ON THE *CREOLE*

In early November 1841, the American slaving ship *Creole* was 11 days into a journey from Virginia to Louisiana. The ship carried a cargo of tobacco and 135 slaves to be sold at the New Orleans slave market. On November 7, 19 slaves, led by a slave named Madison Washington, rose up against the ship's crew, killing one man. The rebels then piloted the boat to Nassau in the Bahamas, a British territory. The British, who had outlawed slavery in 1833, immediately declared the slaves on the *Creole* free. The crew of the *Creole* was then allowed to go to New Orleans with five enslaved people who asked to stay on the ship. It arrived in New Orleans in December.

The news of the mutiny and the British action created an uproar in the United States and other countries. A diplomatic nightmare ensued, with the United States claiming that U.S. "property" should be protected in all foreign ports. After political pressure, the British agreed to pay the slave owners for their lost cargo. However, they refused to return the African Americans to a life of bondage.

Ohio representative Joshua Giddings suggested that the slaves from the *Creole* should remain free once they were outside the United States.

In the U.S. House of Representatives, Joshua Giddings of Ohio said that once outside the United States, the slaves were free and should remain so. Giddings's statement violated the gag order that prevented politicians from talking about slavery in Congress, and he was forced to resign by his colleagues. However, his supporters back home quickly reelected him and sent him back to Washington.

After the *Creole* mutiny, William Ellery Channing, a Boston minister and writer, took the opportunity to speak out against slavery. He published a pamphlet called *The Duty of the Free States, or Remarks Suggested by the Case of the* Creole. In the book, Channing defended the British actions and condemned the practice of slavery:

Madison Washington: A Life of Rebellion

As a slave in Virginia, Madison Washington escaped to freedom in Canada. He returned, however, to free his wife, Susan. He was recaptured and put on board the *Creole* to be sold in Louisiana. A lover of freedom, Washington was also compassionate. It was said that he prevented angry slaves from killing the captain and other crew members and that he tended to the wounds of injured crew men after the mutiny.

Later, Frederick Douglass wrote a fictionalized account of Washington's life and the *Creole* mutiny called *The Heroic Slave*. Douglass compared Washington with America's founding fathers. He described Washington as *"a man who loved liberty as well as did Patrick Henry—who deserved it as much as did Thomas Jefferson—and who fought for it with a valor as high, an arm as strong, and against odds as great, as he who led all the armies of the American colonies through the great war for freedom and independence."*

The first and most essential exercise of love towards a human being, is to respect his Rights. It is idle to talk of kindness to a human being, whose rights we habitually trample underfoot. . . . A human being is not to be loved as a horse or a dog, but as a being having rights; and his first grand right is that of free action; the right to use and expand his powers.

BOLD VOICES IN THE WILDERNESS

In 1843, Henry Highland Garnet rose to speak at the National Negro Convention in Buffalo, New York. As Garnet, a former slave, spoke, gasps and whispers erupted throughout the audience. No black had ever dared to utter in public the words that Garnet now spoke. In his "Call to Rebellion," Garnet urged slaves to rise up in violent rebellion against their white masters:

Brethren, arise, arise! Strike for your lives and liberties. Now is the day and the hour. Let every slave throughout the land do this, and the days of slavery are numbered. You cannot be more oppressed than you have been—you cannot suffer greater cruelties than you have already. Rather die freemen than live to be slaves. Remember that you are FOUR MILLIONS!

Garnet's revolutionary call to action was a failure. Another delegate at the convention, Frederick Douglass, the foremost black abolitionist, spoke out against Garnet's position. Douglass and others believed that the abolition of slavery could come about only through the efforts of white politicians and abolitionists to convince slaveholders that they were morally wrong. The convention allowed Garnet another chance to defend his beliefs. When delegates voted between the two approaches to abolition, Garnet's views were rejected by just one vote.

FIGHTING THE FUGITIVE SLAVE LAW

In 1850, the U.S. Congress passed the Compromise of 1850, a set of laws that tried to satisfy both Southern slaveholders and Northern abolitionists. Lawmakers hoped that the legislation would keep the peace between North and South. Part of the compromise was a new Fugitive Slave Law. The new law gave slave owners more power than the 1793 Fugitive Slave Law had to collect their "property" in Northern states. It also laid out punishments for anyone who harbored or aided a runaway slave.

While many Southerners were pleased with the new Fugitive Slave Law, antislavery forces in the North were not. Almost immediately, abolitionists and others who hated slavery set out to defy the new law. One of the first such acts of defiance occurred in Christiana, Pennsylvania. On September 11, 1851, a Maryland farmer named Edward Gorsuch arrived in town, looking for four of his slaves who had run away. Gorsuch had heard that his slaves were being protected by a freed black man named William Parker. Gorsuch and other slave catchers visited Parker's home with four warrants—one for each runaway slave. The men pushed their way into Parker's home and demanded that the slaves be turned over to them. Gorsuch even tried to rush up Parker's stairs and take the slaves himself.

Parker's wife blew a horn, gathering a crowd of between 75 and 100 free blacks, as well as several white farmers. The slave catchers retreated outside. Gunfire broke out between the two parties. Gorsuch was killed in this attack—clubbed with a pistol, shot by several onlookers, and slashed with sickles. Other members of the posse were beaten and shot but managed to escape from the angry mob.

After the Christiana incident, Parker fled to Canada. He soon found himself in the same position that Gorsuch's four slaves had been in: William F. Johnston, the governor of Pennsylvania, demanded that Parker be returned to the United States. Canada, however, refused to hand him over.

The incident proved that many Northerners were willing to risk violence and death rather than handing over escaped slaves. Frederick Douglass had this to say: "I could not look upon them as murderers. To me, they were heroic defenders of the just right of man against manstealers and murderers." A Cleveland newspaper editorial opined, "This is the first horrible tragedy which has taken place under the Fugitive Slave Law. We had expected such a catastrophe before this; and, we fear, it is but the beginning of a series of riots which will end, as it has begun, in blood."

For Southerners, it was yet another example of the Northern lack of respect for their way of life and their "property rights." Many in the South now felt that a split was inevitable. A Nashville newspaper summed it up: "A crisis has come, this affair will test the matter."

Antislavery forces defied the new law in other states, too. In Massachusetts and New York, black and white abolitionists broke into courtrooms and rescued captured fugitive slaves. In 1851, for example, black men entered a courthouse in Boston and grabbed a fugitive slave named Shadrach Minkins. The men then helped Minkins escape to freedom in Canada.

In the early to mid-1800s, before and during the Civil War, white and black abolitionists would hold antislavery meetings, such as the one shown in this sketch, to discuss what could be done to help bring about slavery's end.

In Boston, the inhumanity of the Fugitive Slave Law was brought to the public's attention by the case of Anthony Burns. As a self-educated slave in Alexandria, Virginia, Burns had enjoyed unusual freedoms that many other slaves did not. For example, his master, Charles Suttle, allowed Burns to hire himself out in his spare time. However, Burns had an overwhelming desire to be his own master. In 1854, he boarded a ship in Richmond headed for Boston and—he thought—freedom.

Burns quickly learned that many Northerners were willing to sacrifice the liberty of escaped slaves in order to obey the Fugitive Slave Law.

Crowds watch as Anthony Burns is led to the Boston, Massachusetts docks where he was placed on a ship and sent back into slavery.

When Suttle followed Burns to Boston, the escaped slave was falsely arrested for a crime he did not commit and thrown in jail.

As Burns sat in jail awaiting trial, black abolitionists decided to march on the courthouse in an effort to convince the judges to free him. White abolitionists, hearing of these plans, joined them. Before long, about 2,000 protesters had gathered outside the courthouse. Some of the black men grabbed a large beam to use as a battering ram. The men attacked the courthouse, but were driven away by deputies. In the course of the struggle, one deputy died of knife wounds.

President Franklin Pierce was determined to see the new law obeyed. He knew that the nation hung in a delicate balance between peace and civil war. He ordered U.S. troops to Boston to guard the courthouse and prevent any further violence.

On June 2, Burns was found by the court to be a fugitive slave and ordered to be sent back to his master in Virginia. On the day Burns was loaded onto a southbound ship, about 50,000 people turned out to watch the man walk in shackles from the courthouse to the docks. The Burns case had a profound effect on how both slave owners and abolitionists viewed the Fugitive Slave Law.

Less than a year after Burns was shipped back to Virginia, a black church in Boston raised $1,300 to purchase him from his master. He returned to Boston, where he had received so much support.

Three years after the Burns case, another court case outraged abolitionists and enemies of slavery. In 1857, the U.S. Supreme Court ruled that no black person, whether enslaved or freed, could be a citizen of the United States. The court's ruling, known as the *Dred Scott* decision, convinced some people that the only way to end slavery was through a violent and bloody uprising.

8

A Country Divided

On October 17, 1859, federal troops closed in on John Brown and his followers at the arsenal at Harpers Ferry, Virginia. Brown thought that only violence could bring about emancipation for the slaves.

BROWN'S REBELLION

John Brown was one American who decided that only a violent revolution would free the slaves. On October 16, 1859, Brown attacked and captured a U.S. armory and arsenal at Harpers Ferry, Virginia. This raid was the climax of a life dedicated to abolition.

Born in Connecticut, Brown had grown up in a religious family that hated slavery. As he aged, he became even more fiercely opposed to the cruel practice. Although Brown himself was never a financial success, he always remained committed to helping those who were without their freedom. For example, Brown helped pay to publish David Walker's *Appeal* and Henry Highland Garnet's "Call to Rebellion." Brown also sheltered and aided runaway slaves.

Some of Brown's earliest recruits were found among his 20 children. In 1856, for example, Brown and some of his sons came to fame as antislavery fighters in Kansas. At this time, "Bleeding Kansas" was a battleground between slavery and antislavery forces. The new territory was about to vote on whether it would become a free or a slave state. Armed Southerners and Northerners poured into the territory, determined to have their way in the upcoming vote. In Kansas, Brown killed five proslavery settlers in revenge for the murders of five antislavery settlers. Brown and his sons later fought in Missouri, another slavery battleground.

Brown's plan to capture the arsenal at Harpers Ferry was the first step in a larger revolt. He believed that once enslaved people heard of his rebellion, they would rise up throughout the South and start a full-scale war against their white oppressors. Brown intended to arm the rebels with the weapons from the captured arsenal. He was aided in his efforts by 21 other men, including a fugitive slave, four free blacks, and two of his sons.

Brown's Rebellion at Harpers Ferry was a failure. In less than two days, U.S. troops led by Robert E. Lee (who later commanded Confederate troops against the Union in the Civil War) killed or captured most of the men. Among the dead were Brown's two sons. Brown himself was seriously wounded. He was put on trial while still injured, lying on a cot in front of the judge. He was quickly found guilty of treason and other crimes.

In this illustration, John Brown cradles one of his dying sons as Robert E. Lee's troops overwhelm the abolitionist and his followers in October 1859.

Brown was sentenced to be hanged on December 2, 1859. In one of his last letters, the 59-year-old man foresaw the coming bloody violence that would be known as the Civil War. He wrote, "I . . . am now quite certain that the crimes of this guilty land will never be purged away but with blood."

After his death, John Brown was considered a martyr for the antislavery cause. The song "John Brown's Body" became a popular marching song for Union soldiers during the Civil War.

Brown's Rebellion helped to convince many Northerners that slavery must be ended at any cost. Abolitionist William Lloyd Garrison, who had at first condemned Brown's violent methods, said after Brown's death that every slaveholder who opposed emancipation "had forfeited his right to live." Brown's revolt—and abolitionist reaction like Garrison's—made Southerners more certain than ever that a split with the North could not be avoided.

TROUBLE IN TEXAS

As Canada was a haven for fugitive slaves from the Deep South, Mexico was a haven for fugitive slaves from Texas. Mexico had abolished slavery in 1835. By the 1850s, an estimated 4,000 escaped slaves lived south of the U.S. border.

The summer of 1860 saw rumors of slave revolt spread throughout the northern part of Texas. Mysterious fires were started in Dallas and other towns at the same time, and newspapers in the region published letters suggesting that abolitionists and slaves were plotting to kill all the whites in northern Texas. White Texans rose up in a panic. Groups of vigilantes captured and questioned slaves and abolitionists in the region. They may have killed between 30 and 100 blacks and whites during their interrogations.

Today, historians believe that the rumors of rebellion that led to the "Texas Troubles" were false. However, the incident had a long-lasting effect. It strongly cemented sentiment against the Northern abolitionists. It also alienated Southerners against Abraham Lincoln, the Republican candidate for president. In 1861, the Texas Troubles were fresh in the minds of many Texans when they voted three to one to secede from the Union.

THE BEGINNING OF THE END

In November 1860, Abraham Lincoln was elected president of the United States. Many Southern states, fearing that Lincoln would try to end slavery, threatened to secede. In December, South Carolina became the first state to follow through on its pledge. The next month, five more Southern states followed. These six states set up a new nation, the Confederate States of America. Jefferson Davis of Mississippi was chosen as president. In the coming months, five more states would join the new Southern nation, bringing its total members to 11.

In April 1861, the smoldering conflict between North and South erupted into outright warfare when Confederate troops fired on Fort Sumter in Charleston's harbor. The Civil War lasted for the next four years, and more than 600,000 Americans would die as a result.

SLAVE REBELLIONS CONTINUE

Slaves who did not run away during the war sometimes took the chance to organize rebellions. Soon after the war broke out, revolts and conspiracies were reported in Arkansas, Kentucky, Mississippi, South Carolina, and Virginia. Cases of arson in the South were often blamed on slaves. In May 1861, for example, 12 ships in New Orleans were destroyed by fires. Seven months later, a fire in Charleston burned 600 buildings to the ground. Slaves were suspected in both cases.

In 1862, slaves marched on New Orleans, attacking the police who tried to stop them. Also in that year, in Adams County, Mississippi, leaders of a planned rebellion were hanged, and their bodies were left to rot in public to deter future troublemakers. Afterward, the governor of Mississippi told Confederate officials that no more fighting men could be spared. They were needed at home to make sure that the slaves did not rise up against their owners.

Confederate officials did their best to keep news of revolts quiet. They did not want this information passed to the North or to slaves in other Confederate states. Throughout the war, slave unrest and violence would disrupt nearly all slaveholding states.

Slaves also became bolder in expressing their opinions. On Christmas Eve in 1861, slaves in New Castle, Kentucky, were reported as parading through town, "singing political songs, and shouting for Lincoln." No one stopped them.

Black Union troops are shown fighting Confederate forces at Petersburg, Virginia, during the Civil War. By the end of the Civil War, 10 percent of the Union army was made up of black soldiers, many of them former slaves.

FIGHTING FOR THE UNION

During the war, many slaves escaped to Union army camps. At first, the escaped slaves were made to do manual labor. This included a variety of tasks, such as setting up camp, digging ditches and trenches, and cooking meals for white soldiers. An estimated 200,000 fugitive slaves helped the Union army in this way. Later, the runaways were given weapons and allowed to fight. The first black regiments were formed in Louisiana and Kansas in 1862.

In the South during the war, groups of runaway slaves and communities of maroons fought their own guerrilla war against the Confederates. In some cases, the slaves were helped by whites who had deserted from the Confederate army. Florida, with its swamps and wild, heavily wooded land, was especially prone to such fighting. Raiding parties often attacked plantations, stealing goods and freeing slaves there. Throughout the war, reports of guerrilla groups, Confederate deserters, and maroons filtered north from the state.

Even slaves still living on their masters' plantations or serving the Confederacy helped the Union forces. According to one source, the slaves "piloted the Union forces, [and] cared for their prisoners when they escaped from the enemy; as spies these Negroes brought valuable information, and hailed the approach of the stars and stripes with wildest demonstrations of joy."

Robert Smalls was a South Carolina slave who served as pilot of the Confederate steamship *Planter*. On the evening of May 12, 1862, the white crew of the *Planter* left the ship in the hands of the nine black crew members and went ashore. Smalls put on the captain's uniform, then steered the boat to a quiet wharf where he smuggled his wife and three children aboard. Early the next morning, Smalls turned the ship around and headed out of Charleston Harbor, sailing right past the big guns of Fort Sumter. He turned the ship over to Union blockade ships outside the harbor.

Born into slavery in South Carolina, Robert Smalls worked near the ocean in Charleston from the age of 12, first loading and unloading cargo and then making sails. Later, Smalls served as a deckhand and pilot aboard Carolina ships.

After turning the ship *Planter* over to the Union army and escaping to the North during the Civil War, Smalls fought for the Union, eventually becoming a captain in the Union navy. Following the war, Smalls returned to South Carolina. In the coming years, he served five terms in Congress, representing South Carolina and championing equal treatment for blacks in the United States.

THE END OF SLAVERY

On January 1, 1863, President Lincoln issued the Emancipation Proclamation. This decree freed slaves in states that were in open rebellion against the Union. (It did not free slaves in states that had remained loyal to the Union or were under Union control.) The proclamation also allowed blacks to sign up and fight for Union forces.

The last known slave rebellion conspiracy was uncovered in December 1864 in Troy, Alabama. The plot was said to include slaves, deserters from the Confederate army, and escaped Union prisoners. In April 1865, the South surrendered, and the Civil War came to an end. Eight months later, the Thirteenth Amendment to the U.S. Constitution was passed. The amendment finally made slavery illegal within the United States. The fight for freedom was over, but blacks still faced a long struggle for equality and respect.

Time Line

1522	The first known slave revolt in the Americas takes place on the island of Hispaniola.
1526	The first slave revolt on the mainland of North America occurs at the Spanish colony of San Miguel de Gualdape.
1600	Slaves in Brazil overthrow Portuguese masters in Pernambuco.
1665	The first slave revolt in the British North American colonies takes place in Gloucester County, Virginia.
1712	A slave rebellion in New York City results in the deaths of about 12 whites and numerous slaves.
1726	Slaves in Suriname begin a decades-long rebellion against their Dutch masters.
1730	One of the first recorded slave mutinies aboard a slaving ship takes place on the *Little George,* a Rhode Island vessel.
1733	Slaves revolt on St. John in the Virgin Islands, killing one-third of the Danish colonists there.
1739	The Stono Rebellion, the largest and deadliest slave revolt in the history of colonial North America, takes place in South Carolina, resulting in the deaths of about 21 whites and twice as many slaves.

1741	Fires in New York City are blamed on slaves; more than 30 are executed, and many more are banished from the colony.
1763	A huge rebellion takes place in Berbice, a Dutch colony on South America's northeast coast.
1775	Lord Dunmore decrees that any slave who deserts an American master to fight for the British will be freed.
1791	The only successful slave rebellion in the Americas begins in the French colony on the island of Hispaniola. Slaves will eventually overthrow the white colonists on the entire island and form the republic of Haiti.
1793	The first Fugitive Slave Law is passed by the U.S. Congress.
1800	Gabriel's Rebellion, the largest insurrection yet seen in the United States, shocks Southerners in Richmond, Virginia.
1811	The largest slave revolt in U.S. history takes place in the Louisiana Territory.
1816	Three hundred runaway slaves and about 30 American Indians take control of Fort Blount, an abandoned British fortress in Apalachicola Bay. There is also a slave rebellion in Barbados.
1820	Congress passes the Missouri Compromise.
1822	A rebellion led by Denmark Vesey is betrayed and halted before it can start.
1829	David Walker issues his *Appeal* to blacks in the United States.

1831	Nat Turner's Rebellion results in the deaths of about 55 whites and more than 100 blacks. Jamaica's Great Slave Revolt takes place.
1833	Great Britain's Parliament votes to abolish slavery in its colonies.
1839	Slaves rebel on board the Spanish slaver *Amistad*.
1841	Slaves on board the *Creole* rise up, overwhelm the crew members, and force them to sail to the Bahamas, where almost all the slaves are freed.
1850	Congress passes another Fugitive Slave Law.
1851	Residents in Christiana, Pennsylvania, violently defend fugitive slaves from Southern slave catchers.
1859	John Brown's unsuccessful revolt increases the fears of rebellion in slaveholders in the South.
1861	The Civil War begins.
1863	President Abraham Lincoln issues the Emancipation Proclamation.
1864	The last known slave conspiracy is discovered, in Troy, Alabama.

Glossary

abolitionist   A person who seeks an immediate end to slavery.

cooper   A barrel maker.

Deep South   Usually refers to the part of the United States that includes Alabama, Arkansas, Florida, Georgia, Louisiana, Mississippi, Texas, and parts of the Carolinas and Tennessee.

emancipation   The act of freeing slaves.

fugitive   A person who escapes from slave owners or law officials.

guerrilla   An independent fighter who use raids and ambushes to attack the enemy.

indenture   A contract that requires a person to work for a master for a certain number of years.

insurrection   A rebellion or uprising.

Loyalist   An American who supported the British during the American Revolution.

maroons   Fugitive slaves who started their own communities in remote areas.

mutiny   Rebellion, especially aboard a ship.

Parliament   Great Britain's lawmaking body.

Patriot   A person who supported freedom from Great Britain during the American Revolution.

petition   A written request to a person in authority.

plantation   A large farm that relied on slaves to produce one main crop.

prejudice   An unreasonable bias against or intolerance of others.

racism   Prejudice based on race.

secede   To break away from a larger group or government and become independent.

Thirteenth Amendment   An amendment to the U.S. Constitution prohibiting slavery.

warrant   A legal document that allows a law officer to arrest someone.

West Indies   A group of islands in the Caribbean Sea.

Further Reading

BOOKS

Grant, R. G. *The African-American Slave Trade.* Hauppauge, N.Y.: Barron's Educational Series, 2002.

Katz, William Loren. *Breaking the Chains: African-American Slave Resistance.* New York: Aladdin Paperbacks, 1998.

Rossi, Ann. *Freedom Struggle: The Anti-Slavery Movement, 1830–1865.* Washington, D.C.: National Geographic Library, 2005.

Taylor, Yuval. *Growing Up in Slavery: Stories of Young Slaves as Told by Themselves.* Chicago: Lawrence Hill Books, 2005.

Zeinert, Karen. *The* Amistad *Slave Revolt and American Abolition.* North Haven, Conn.: Linnet Books, 1997.

WEB SITES

Anti-Slavery International, UNESCO, the British Council, and NORAD. "Breaking the Silence: Learning about the Transatlantic Slave Trade." URL: http://www.anti slavery.org/breakingthesilence/. Downloaded on August 11, 2005.

The Library of Congress. "African-American Odyssey." URL: http://lcweb2.loc.gov/ammem/aaohtml/aohome.html. Downloaded on August 11, 2005.

Mystic Seaport. "Exploring *Amistad* at Mystic Seaport." URL: http://amistad.mystic seaport.org/. Downloaded on August 11, 2005.

New York Life Insurance Company. "Slavery in America: The History of Slavery in America." URL: http://www.slaveryinamerica.org/history/overview.htm. Downloaded on August 11, 2005.

Index